ALCHEMY OF THE GODS

OCCULTISM IN NORTHERN MYTHOLOGY

C.E. McCann

Copyright ©C.E. McCann

All rights reserved. No part of this book may be reproduced or used in any manner without the express written permission of the publisher except for the use of brief quotations in a book review. All images within this book are property of The Three Little Sisters and may not be duplicated without permission from the publisher.

ISBN13: 978-1-959350-58-3

Set in: Georgia 10/11/16 pt, Trismegistus 17/24 pt

©The Three Little Sisters
USA/CANADA

For SG, SR and VP, may you go further than I have.

For RP, the most amazing Goði, mentor and partner I could have asked for.

For my kindred, you all have made me better.

For Odin, he knows why.

Contents

Fundamentals of esoteric alchemy	14
Fundamentals of numerology	22
Fundamentals of esoteric geometry	25
The valknut	27
The black sun	28
Fundamentals of rune work	30
Fehu	35
Uruz	37
Thurisaz	39
Ansuz	40
Raidho	42
Kenaz	43
Gebo	44
Wunjo	45
Hagalaz	46
Nauthiz	47
Isa	48
Jera	49
Eihwaz	50
Perthro	51
Elhaz	53
Sowilo	54
Tiwaz	55
Berkano	56
Ehwaz	57
Mannaz	58
Laguz	59
Ingwaz	60
Dagaz	61
Othala	62
Alchemical rune work	64
Step one-Nauthiz – identification of need	69
Step two-Hagalaz – objective breakdown	69
Step three-Eihwaz – conversing with the shadow	70
Step four-Gebo – exchanging transference for understanding	71
Step five-Isa – hardening and integrating the shadow	72
Step six-Ingwaz – gestation	72
Step seven-Sowilo – the will refined	73
Step eight-Dagaz – coagulation of day and night	74
Step nine-Jera – the erilaz and the harvest	74
Alchemy in the lore	75
The infinite gods	81

INTRODUCTION

Everything in existence, from the changing of seasons to the process of human reproduction involves a form of alchemy. When we process information, when we take in new ideas and formulate opinions and understanding based on what we are presented with, we are, in a way, alchemists. We break down the bigger idea into pieces we can consume and absorb. After that, we rearrange these bits and construct an individualized understanding.

Summer brings warmth and the ability for plants to grow with greater ease. As we know, photosynthesis comes from the sun and during summer, the sun is at its peak. Autumn breaks these organic materials down to feed the Earth and last the cold months in wintertime. Spring revitalizes our surroundings and births a new generation of material. The process afterward repeats infinitely. When someone becomes pregnant, the body weakens to support the growth of another human being. It breaks and stretches to the limit and a new being emerges. Once you see the alchemical process in the base level human experience and in natural phenomena, you will begin to notice it everywhere and in everything. Dissolving and coagulating our understanding of magic repeatedly will lead to a hardened view and a deeper knowledge of how magic works.

Historically, alchemy was thought of as a tangible, scientific study. It is the grandfather of modern chemistry, after all. With traditional alchemy there are seven stages. The end result of traditional alchemy being sometimes referred to as the Philosopher's Stone or the Elixir of Life. The Chinese alchemists called it the Golden Pill and in the west it was called "the tincture". The first step is calcination, the burning of the material until it's reduced to ash. Second is dissolution, dissolving the ashes made from calcination in water (or acid or another fluid). The third step is separation. Separation is where the components of dissolution are isolated by filtration; It is the separation of the needed and the unneeded. Step four is conjunction, where we recombine the pure leftovers from the previous stages into something of value. Fifth is putrefaction or fermentation. The fifth stage is where the material leftovers are allowed to rot. The material will turn black and eventually turn to yellow ferment.

The Peacock Stage (detail), attributed to Jorg Breu the Elder, (German, ca. 1475-1537). Miniature from the illuminated manuscript Splendor solis oder Sonneglanz, fol. 28r, 1531-32. Staaliche Museen zu Berlin, Kupferstichkabinett, Cod. 78 D 3

Before the act of fermentation, the putrefaction comes to an end with the Peacock's Tail. This is sometimes referred to as the peacock stage or chemical rainbow. When the rotting material will turn iridescent as opposed to the black seen with putrefaction. Six is distillation, this is where the fermented solution is boiled and increased in purity. The last stage, stage seven is coagulation, this is where the focus material is solidified. This is the unification of all aspects involved to create the final material or understanding. The four-stage alchemical process differs slightly but essentially is the seven stages condensed. These are the blackening (Nigredo), the whitening (Albedo), the yellowing (Citrinitas) and the reddening (Rubedo). In Jungian terms these are confession, illumination, education and transformation.

An 1856 depiction of the Sabbatic Goat from Dogme et Rituel de la Haute Magie by Eliphas Levi. The arms bear the Latin words SOLVE (disosolve) and COAGULA (coagulate).

Some interpretations of these four stages vary a little. Some equate them with the four elements or cardinal directions. Equating these with the elements or directions can serve as a way to remember them as well as allow them to be used in magical workings. For example, if you're focused on the blackening phase, it can help you to maintain that alchemical and magical state of mind if you face a certain direction while you study or meditate. The Greek pre-Socratic philosopher Empedocles was the first to establish the four elements making up the structure of the world. He equated them with Zeus, Hera, Nestis and Aidoneus. These could be understood as the dwarves Northri, Austri, Vestri and Suthri as far as directions, or as any of the Æsir or Vanir Gods.

According to archeology and non-magical history, there is no evidence to support the usage of the elder futhark for magical purposes. There is nothing to support the usage of bind runes for magical purposes either. However, we know from the lore that Odin, after sacrificing his eye at Mimir's Well and hanging himself by his spear Gungnir, gained the knowledge of the runes. This is inarguably an allegory for the alchemical process. When we think of sacrifice as an act of relinquishing something that's valued, it is followed by receiving something viewed as greater in value. Sacrifice in this sense is combined with the breaking down or destruction of something and in return, receiving something much more important. In this situation the sacrifice is Odin himself. This sacrifice led to a greater understanding, a new knowledge. This is the meaning behind solve et coagula, the words we see on the forearms of the Baphomet. Separate to join together.

We must break the old to build the new. When studying traditional alchemy and esoteric alchemy, especially while having a set religious belief system, it's not uncommon to be met with boisterous concerns of historical integrity. Some believe it to be sacrilegious to equate the lore many of us grew up hearing with alchemical processes. While it is important to not cheapen the exoteric and esoteric meanings of the runes and the stories, using thought techniques and esoteric teachings from others to better understand our own path is not a detriment. With any aspect of polytheism, or theism in general, it's important to learn the similarities but keep the differences in mind.

While Odin can be connected to Shiva, Hermes, Zeus, Jupiter, or whatever deity he shares attributes with, they are not him and he is not them. There is a benefit in connecting those shared characteristics and being able to see Odin in other theistic practices but, the ability to do so while maintaining his specific nature and being as the Allfather, the Chieftain in Germanic polytheism without making him completely universal is important and absolutely necessary. Having access to and using the practices and conclusions met by other occultists to better understand yourself and your own personal practice is wise. They have paved the way and without them, we wouldn't know the majority of what we do. Hermes Trismegistus, John Dee, Manly P. Hall, Aleister Crowley, even some of the more modern noteworthy and inarguably valuable men like Anton LaVey, have all helped to pave the road of esoteric knowledge and without whom our magical understandings would be severely lacking.

While it is not necessary to agree with any of these men on a personal or moral level, it is willful ignorance to reject everything they've done and said based solely on emotion and personal bias. To have access to people more experienced than yourself is not a threat but a gift. Accessing with ease the conglomeration of centuries of academic and occult study, being able to sit comfortably while reading the life's work of our esoteric forefathers should not be taken for granted. It is with all these ideas, academic works and thought patterns, the amalgamation of my own two decades of occult research that I say this; When you ignore the foundation, the groundwork, you destroy the chances of ever building a strong roof. You therefore choose to build a gold altar, a monument to wisdom upon sand rather than stone or the bones of greater beings than yourself.

Replacing a femur with a yew-branch because the symbolism fits you better doesn't make you wise, it makes you crippled. Do not throw the baby out with the bathwater. It's a valuable skill to have if you can learn to take bits of knowledge and wisdom from every source you come across. You'll find that even the most unlikely source will have some kernel of truth and wisdom if you allow yourself to access it and grasp its concepts.

While all information digested throughout your lifetime has an effect on your thought patterns, each bit of them resting in the subconscious, for the purpose of this little work we will be using just a few. The teachings of Hermeticism, mystic psychology or psycho-spiritualism, alchemy and a form of Jungian psychology. Using these philosophies, we can learn the exoteric and esoteric meanings of the lore, magic and the elder futhark runes. Then, break down our own understandings of them and their meanings and physical makeups and remake them using the conclusions we've come to through these forms of thought which will bring us to a new height in magical thinking and understanding.

While personally I adhere to a physical theistic practice that is almost entirely based on the traditional rites and structures of Germanic Odinic paganism, my internal metaphysical beliefs are slightly different. I am first and foremost an occultist and knowledge seeker. I don't claim to be infallible, nor would I want anyone reading my work to rely solely on my interpretations and conclusions for philosophical or metaphysical wisdom.

One of the wonderful aspects of occult theory is the plethora of viewpoints. The growing interest in spirituality is a double-edged sword. Many don't want to put in the work or find out how the metaphorical sausage is made. To understand the popular concepts today, the semi-commonly known symbols, rituals, numbers and universal allegorical figures or statements, searching and researching is imperative.

Symbolism is the language of the universe; From the microcosm to the macrocosm, from spoken word to written language, every physical aspect of life is coded in this hidden (occult) symbolism. Even symbols as seemingly ordinary as the square, triangle, star or circle have layers of various hidden meanings. Nothing is as it seems.

We stand at the precipice of a promising revival. The thirst for esoteric knowledge increasingly grows within contemporary heathen society as well as many occult circles. A great awakening is growing, it's shedding its skin and unclenching its jaw, its hunger pains are being heard and felt worldwide. We, as pagans, heathens, witches, occultists or any other label we self-bestow have some choices to make. Novice magicians flow in daily and they search for a cup to fill. Those of us who have decades of magical practice under our metaphorical belt can either hide our cups away, forcing newcomers to create cheap knockoffs that easily break, or we can offer ours freely and share among fellow practitioners.

Much of this problem is due to the fact that roots need to form before the tree can withstand a storm. A tree with shallow roots will fall over when the first strong wind passes through. However, when roots are allowed to take hold and grow deep and wide, that tree will be the one still standing while the others have fallen. The point of this book is to give the reader the tools they need to grow their roots. People will try to sell you snake oil and promise that you'll become a Vitki or Völva after just ten easy payments of some substantial amount of money. They will spoon feed you their regurgitated, incorrect information based on other divination forms like tarot. I won't promise you'll be any different after you've read this book, however. What you put into it is what you'll get from it. If you choose to use it as a reference book, that's understandable. If you choose to use it to stop that wobbly chair in your dining room, may your will be done. If you follow its instructions and guides, however, and put your best effort in, you will learn something.

Where do you want to be in five, ten years? Having the same basic conversations about the exoteric meaning of Fehu being cattle? Do you still want to be wondering what else there is to these mysteries? If the runes go deeper than their stave shape? Why did our ancestors believe so deeply in magic and the power of runes if they didn't work but could, by trial and error, create complex tactical movement in war, houses, weapons and ships? Or do you want to connect the runes to your psyche, embed them in your subconscious and feel connected to them on a deeper level? The work you do today, this week, this month will pay off later. Study and understand now so you aren't filled with regret over unfinished work on your deathbed. What a shame it would be to come to the end of your life and feel unfulfilled.

This book is your first step. It can be, if you allow it, the opening to a lifelong, enlightening path that will be as wonderful as it is educational. I implore you, after reading this introductory rune book, search out every written piece available on runes. Some will be noticeably incorrect, some will be difficult to understand, some may change your life. The important thing is to read and study and seek knowledge. Looking at available information objectively and forming your own conclusions is the way forward. Not everything needs to be internalized and not every book you read will have deep truths in them. However, there is a bit of knowledge in everything you read, whether it is applicable or not.

It is my sincerest hope with writing this book that it serves well as a tool for your personal psychospiritual Yggdrasil. I hope there's something here that makes runes click and sets you on the glorious runic path that I love so much. Every witch or occultist has that one book that made all the other books fall into place with ease and I hope this book will either be that or lead you to that book.

FUNDEMENTALS OF ESOTERIC ALCHEMY

The main goal of alchemy is to turn base metals into gold. Now, many have claimed to have accomplished this feat and the results are arguable and lacking in evidence. In modern times, it was discovered that through nuclear transmutation with a particle accelerator, lead can be turned into gold. However, this is not through alchemy. Among the many names involved in the early alchemical ideas and theories are Nicholas Flammel, Paracelsus of Hohenheim, Raymond Lully, John Dee and many others.

There are also many who believe King Solomon and Pythagoras were alchemists and of course, we have the legends of Hermes Trismegistus. Albert Pike, the famous (or infamous) Freemason, author of 'Morals and Dogma' also believed alchemy was not just a philosophical theory, but a tangible science. Alchemy, along with astrology, are the most ancient sciences we know of. As long as humans have existed in the manifest world, we've looked to the sky and the material for answers to life's mysteries.

Alchemy was so widespread in ancient times that we see glimmers of it with the Babylonians, Phœnicians, ancient Europe as well as ancient Egypt. The word "alchemy" even offering a subtle head-nod in Egypt's direction as khem is the ancient word for Egypt. "Al" being a divine prefix as we see in the words "Allah" or "Alohim" in reference to a divine creator entity alone gives us an etymological 'leg' to stand on when we say alchemy is a spiritual practice as opposed to a physical 'scientific' one.

Egypt is also where we meet the figure of Thoth, (believed to be the Egyptian equivalent of Hermes Trismegistus) for the first time. Hermes shares many attributes with other deities given the role of bringing the arts and sciences to the world and was eventually believed to be one in the same. We can see many of these traits in European deities such as Hermod or even Bragi. As far as runes, we can see these attributes in Ansuz, Laguz and even Eihwaz (See chapter on alchemical runology).

The alchemy of the Middle Ages developed into a theistic path which we now see a reemergence of in modern times in some of the new-age circles, sans study and research most of the time. It's important to note that when studying medieval literature, symbolism in writing is not unique to alchemy. It was the popular way of writing at the time so, there is no proof that alchemy, when it started, was a spiritual theory. However, if we look at Jungian psychology, the understanding of alchemical texts through the lens of esotericism is valid. The early modern period and Middle Ages are steeped in symbolic writing. Another important aspect to keep in mind is there was no dogma with traditional alchemy when it came about.

It developed into a theistic practice later on with Jung and Meister Eckhart, but the original alchemists frequently debated and disagreed with each other. Even at its inception, alchemy could not be agreed upon as a practice or theory. Largely, it was pseudoscience. It went from a sulphur and mercury theory, to sulfur, mercury and salt with Paracleus in the 16th century. Paracleus ended up being responsible for alchemy changing in not only theory and methodology, but its goals as well. The transmutation of metals became medicinal transmutation and pharmaceutics.

We also see a familiar theory for Paracleus that resonates with the Germanic or European polytheist. Paracleus believed that mankind was made from a physical body, the soul as an eternal body and a divine spark called 'spiritus' that was regenerated or given through Christ during baptism. We see a similar idea when Odin, Vili and Ve give Ask and Embla breath of life, consciousness and appearance respectively. This continued to transform within Catholicism and eventually this, among other theories deemed wrong and sacrilegious, was debated and tackled by the Protestant Reformation and we see sola fide or faith alone as a belief.

Spiritual alchemy is not unique to any culture, just as traditional alchemy is not. The regenerative process of being born again in Christian theistic beliefs is one that holds weight in many spiritualities, though usually not in the same way. Whereas the Christian believes they've become a completely new being through their God, many others believe they become a better being, or a higher being through a similar process.

We see this same concept with Christ-Consciousness (God-consciousness, Odian or Odinic-consciousness etc.) where the process of rebirth doesn't destroy the old but transforms it. There is some Protestant mysticism or new forms of Gnosticism that believe this to be alchemical allegory as well. Where the Bible is an alchemical text, Christ is the ultimate alchemist and the goal of life is to do what they believed Christ did; become one with their God through transmutation. These theories from the fringe Protestants became a more popular theory in the late 1500s and developed into the idea that Christ is literally the Philosopher's Stone and can then be used to transmute man.

This, along with the Lutheran ideas of salvation being something that man achieves solely through faith, was consistently argued against by the Catholic Church, as it meant the eucharist, rituals and priests and the Church herself were unnecessary for salvation. Later, esoteric alchemical theories began to gain traction in the Germanic world. In the 18th century, we see theories emerge concerning numerology and alchemy with Azoth and Fire, where the number 666 is taken to not mean the Beast, but instead Christ. This theory reemerges in modern gnostic circles focused on eschatology, so, while the original 18th century text is obscure and odd, the idea is not one that's unheard of. This text continues on the same theory of Christ being the Philosopher's Stone.

Numerological significance concerning the number 666 will be explained in the chapter on numerology, but the theory of 666 meaning something divine rather than destructive isn't far off from some modern occult thinkers. This is the grandfatherly theory of modern Christian idea of 'being born again'. There are other texts from the same time period that suggest a transformation of man through Christ with death and rebirth called Divine Alchemy. This is thought of as a literal process that changes the soul of man, whereas the term Divine Alchemy in other medieval literature isn't necessarily speaking as literally.

Later with texts such as Wasserstein Der Weisen written in 1599 by Lucas Jennis, more so popularizes the link between the physical alchemical science and spiritual alchemy. It continues on with the theory that the story of Christ is viewed by the wise as an alchemical one. Therefore, it is one alchemists should look to as an exemplary model of their spiritual goals. So, spiritual alchemy becomes the norm and not only as a later understanding of physical alchemy.

This theory is part of where esoteric alchemy becomes more of a solidified belief system, not only within Abrahamic or Christian circles, but others as well. However, its origins are deeply rooted in Christian mysticism. One can argue otherwise, stating that these spiritual alchemical thinkers of the late Middle Ages through the 18th centuries claiming to be Christians or Catholics were never truly that, rather occultists. One can say these theories are included in every religion and it was always meant to be an esoteric thought, similar to how Jung viewed alchemy as projection of the alchemist.

History and academia show us though, that traditional alchemy was meant to be a real science. However, for the purposes of using the spiritual alchemical process, we can make the philosophical argument that esotericism was and is the backbone of alchemy and for a spiritual process, side with Jung for now. This idea of becoming one with God trickles down through Hermeticism and into Thelema with the emergence of Aleister Crowley.

While it's mostly agreed upon that Crowley wasn't a pillar of moral strength, to put it kindly, Thelema is worth taking a look at if discussing theories on uniting man with God. We see the unicursal hexagram as a geometrical testament to this idea as well as some beliefs surrounding the pentagram, which will be covered in the chapter on geometry. Many occultists aim to become united or at least on the same metaphysical playing-field as God(s). This idea isn't unique to Thelema, though it is a bit more obvious within that belief system.

This is where esoteric alchemy comes into play. Esoteric alchemy can be best understood using John Dee's terminology "The quaternary is concealed within the ternary", meaning the four is in the three. Or the manifest is in the hidden (occult). In Christian terms, this is the world or four major elements within the trinity (Father, Son, Holy Ghost). In European paganism, this is the material world being created by Odin, Villi and Ve.

One of the most influential and important pieces of alchemical history is undoubtedly The Emerald Tablet of Hermes. There's a lot of debate among scholars as to its origin. Some say its earliest version is from the 7th century, written in Arabic. Others claim it was found in Egypt much earlier. All we know for certain is that it's ancient and clearly an allegory for the alchemical formula. There are many translations available, which the reader should compare and contrast, this is just one.

This is the truth, the whole truth and nothing but the truth.
The below is that of the above and the above is that of the below. With this knowledge alone, you may work miracles as done by the one. Through the adaptation of one manifestation.
The sun is its father, the moon is its mother.
The wind carries it in its belly.
And the earth nursed it.
It is the father of all things in the universe, its power is perfect, after it has been united to a spiritous earth.

Separate that spirituous earth from the crude by means of gentle heat.
It rises from the earth and descends again from the heavens, born again. The superior and the inferior are increased in power.
By means of this one thing, all the glory of the world shall be yours
Obscurity will flee from you.
It is the strength of all power.
For it will penetrate all mysteries and dispel all ignorance In this way the world was created, the way to follow this road is hidden. It is for this reason I am called Hermes Trismegistus; for I possess the three essentials of the philosophy of the universe.
This is the sum total of the work of the Sun.

Here, we see that alchemy is very much intertwined with theism. It teaches that the one, God, the creator(s) or the trinity, is within everything. If we view Odin, Villi and Ve as a trinity, which many occultists believe them to be, this is saying that Odinic trinity, that threefold creator-God is in everything. Within and without. This is one interpretation of the mysteries surrounding the 33rd degree in Freemasonry. 33 = 3x3=9. Nine, as will be discussed in the chapter on Numerology is one of the, if not the most important number in numerology in general, but especially European Pagan numerology.

Growth or expansion is another important aspect of alchemy. Many will say that for alchemy to be a reality, it must create something from nothing, which we know to be impossible. Energy cannot be created or destroyed, as the first law of thermodynamics states. As with the scientific idea of causal determinism, nothing in the universe has no cause or is self-caused.

The alchemist instead purports to improve upon nature, or at least be able to recreate it himself. "You may work miracles as done by the one." Esoterically this is understood as becoming one with God or obtaining Odian (God)-consciousness. The act of ascending from lower states of consciousness to a higher state of consciousness. Turning lead into gold, the raw self into the higher self. Through esoteric alchemy, take the ignorant man and transmute him into a God.

If the above is that of the below, meaning not merely reflections of one another but one in the same, then they are the same material at opposite extreme points. Similar to extreme heat and cold, they vary in temperature but not in severity. If these things are true, it only stands to reason that man is the microcosm, God(s) being the macrocosm. Furthermore, the ideas of some of the occult forefathers that the stars and man are connected isn't a great leap of faith. We know at least this is somewhat attested to in the lore as Odin, Villi and Ve created man and woman from Ash and Elm. Clearly another symbolic attestation for the interconnectedness of man and nature.

When we understand that the sentience of man has the ability to be that of the Gods, that nature is connected to every immaterial and material aspect of the cosmos, we understand that the superior and the inferior are increased in power. They agree with each other on their cause and their effect. This theory is not unique to any path, however. It can align with every belief system known to us. It reconciles with them all. It may be considered sacrilegious to the pious, but it remains intellectually valid, nonetheless.

There are a great many occultists who believe that alchemy was always a metaphysical and philosophical art. At the height of alchemical innovation and thought, the penalties for writing, reading or speaking in a way deemed reprobate or in league with witchcraft could land one in prison or worse. The 16th century was saturated with accusations of witchcraft and fingers pointing at Satan for any ill fortune. In 1542, UK Parliament passed what was called the Witchcraft Act which made witchcraft a crime punishable by death. This was when the famous mathematician and occultist John Dee was just fifteen years old. During the Late Middle Ages (14th century) during the time of Nicolas Flamel, those accused of witchcraft were still being burned at the stake. It wouldn't have taken much to be accused of sorcery during this time, thus it stands to reason that any form of occult thought, Gnosticism or esotericism would need to be concealed behind a lens of science or mathematics.

We know that these alchemists, mathematicians, astronomers and philosophers were not unintelligent, and we can reasonably assume that they wouldn't all be liars. So then, what other reasoning would a fairly large group of intelligent people have to claim to be able to turn lead into gold through the alchemical process? Occultism is the answer, esoteric alchemy is the key. We see hints of it in many famous literary and artistic works.

Looking at alchemy through the lens of spirituality, we can make the connections between the statements seen in these writings and magical transformation or spellwork. Therefore, we can reasonably use alchemical thinking as a spiritual working. Turning lead to gold is turning the raw self or the raw rune into the highest self or the highest understanding of a rune. The self and the runes we can break down and view objectively, come to new realizations about, become fully aware and in tune with these new illuminating conclusions and use these conclusions to transform ourselves and our understanding into something new and better.

This process is much like shadow work when done with yourself as the focus, which we will get into later. Refining yourself, identifying triggers and emotional barriers and admitting to yourself what your weaknesses are is the first part. Using these insights about yourself to better yourself is the goal. When you know what piece of a machine is broken, you have an idea of where to begin in order to have it working at top efficiency again. When you know what parts of yourself need to be addressed and acknowledged, you can begin to tame these parts and have them benefit you rather than hinder you.

This process for both the self and the runes are done similarly but, in order to understand the runes in the deepest way you can, you must understand yourself in the deepest way possible first. Herein lies the issues many face with their personal practices and studies. The reason why spells won't work, wards won't work, and runes aren't doing what the user wants, is because they do not understand themselves.

We know that as far as has been studied and proven, a tangible Philosopher's Stone does not exist, and the Elixir of Life is not based in reality. The fountain of youth is, as far as we can show, a myth. However, as with many stories and aims of the scientists, philosophers and academics of antiquity, alchemy is shrouded in mystic language, occult truths and esoteric mysteries. From its symbolism to the three primary elements being salt, sulphur and mercury, we see that we can take the esoteric meanings from the wording meant to conceal these teachings. A brief overview of these elements and their human correspondences are salt for the body, mercury for the spirit or mind, and sulphur for the soul.

Now, with alchemy, these three, body, spirit/mind and soul are not necessarily thought of in the modern sense as their meanings are derived, in this sense, from Hermeticism. Some believe that they could also represent other ideas as well. Salt being the earth, sulphur being a spiritual fire and mercury being a representation of the God Hermes. Either understanding brings us to a similar conclusion however and both are equally as helpful moving forward. For us, when thinking in terms of Germanic and Norse polytheism, Mercury can easily be thought of as representing Odin.

So, knowing the Philosopher's Stone and the elixir of life are not physical objects, knowing the relations others have made to the earth or spirituality, what are they when it comes to their usage for spiritual alchemy in the physical plane for the purpose of this book? Just as the occultist or practitioner is the force behind the magic, the mind of the occultist is the Philosopher's Stone, while the spirit of the occultist is the elixir of life.

FUNDEMENTALS OF NUMEROLOGY

There is no debate that all myths and religions attribute divine meaning to numbers. We see number associations for letters throughout almost every ancient alphabet. The word alphabet itself being the first and second letters of the Greek and Hebrew alphabets. Alpha being the first letter in the Greek alphabet, Aleph being the first in the Hebrew. Beta being second for the Greek and Beth being the second for the Hebrew. The etymology of the word alphabet comes from the Greek words alpha and beta, later the Latin word alphabetum and then alphabet in the early 16th century.

The practice of numerology, known as arithmancy prior to the 20th century, has been reconciled with almost all religions since, though contemporary Christians are still wary about using math to understand faith. This didn't seem to be a problem for the 16th century Italian Catholic and academic, Pietro Bongo. Author of Numerorum Mysteria (1591) he attempted to use Pythagorean mathematics with Christian theology. We see that numerology is used throughout Christian mythology, even without a belief in numerology as an occult practice.

In Revelation, the author tells the reader to count or calculate the number of the beast, which is also the number of man being 666. With numerology, we see 6+6+6=18 and 1+8=9. We then see in Revelation that 144,000 will be saved. 1+4+4=9. There again we see the number 9 having great importance within destruction and creation. The trinity, the number of days it took for the Christian God to create the world, etc.

We see numerological significance throughout Northern European myths as well and the significance changes only slightly between European myths, Egyptian, and the Abrahamic myths. In the lore we see a trinity of God(s) that created the world along with man and woman. We see the three Norns, somewhat similar to the three Greek fates. The three containers of the mead of poetry, Othrörir.

The three ættir in the Elder Futhark and how we use the first three letters in the Latin alphabet when we reference it ABC, and so on. It is obvious that numbers play a significant role in our life. For the purpose of this book, we will base the numerology we use on symbolism in the lore for a numerological method that works better in a Northern European context. The numerology key as follows will outline the significance of numbers from here on.

Number	Examples
ONE signifies beginnings and solitary forces.	Ginungagap and Yggdrasil.
TWO symbolizes cooperation and teamwork between forces, whether for creative force or destructive.	Hugin and Mugin, Geri and Freki, Skol and Hati, Arvakr and Alsvidhr, Muspelheim and Niflheim.
THREE is a trinity or a creative function.	THREE is a trinity or a creative function.
FOUR represents powerful solidity and solar attributes.	The four dwarves, Austri, Vestri, Norðri and Suðri. The solar wheel and swastika as symbols of Thor.
FIVE signifies natural space and time.	The ancient Germanic week was five nights long and was called a fimmt.
SIX is representative of strength.	The six external points of the valknut
SEVEN represents death and travel.	Seven traditional nights between death and funeral rites. The rainbow traditionally has seven colors.
EIGHT is the representation of the fruit of manifestation and symmetry.	Eight runes in each of the ættir, Slepnir's eight legs.
NINE is completion, it represents the magician and Odin, transformation and eternalness.	Nine worlds, 9 nights Odin hung, 9 points total on the Valknut, Draupnir reproducing every ninth night. Heimdall's nine mothers, the nine daughters of Rán and Ægir, the nine locks on Surt's sword. Groa's nine spells as well as there are also nine parts of the soul complex.

These certainly aren't definitive and could and should be expounded upon and debated. They are, however, a good starting block for understanding various myths and ideas through numerology. Now, if we take these numerological ideas and compare and contrast them with those of other cultures and understandings of numbers, we can understand much more about the significance of numbers in myths and legends.

FUNDEMENTALS OF ESOTERIC GEOMETRY

While geometry is the study of special properties such as distance, shape, size and position; Sacred Geometry is the belief that geometrical shapes that are repeated in the manifest world have divine meaning. These are the fundamental shapes and patterns that govern all life. Throughout occult history these shapes have been regarded as symbols of some of life's greatest mysteries and truths.

When we look at the spirals on the nautilus shell, or the pattern of the petals on a flower, crystals, snowflakes, beehives and tree trunks, we see that geometry and nature are irrevocably linked. The human body is another natural testament to the interconnected geometrical structure that shapes the material world. From the veins in our hands to the gyri and sulci of the brain, down to the shape of our DNA, we are full of sacred geometry.

These shapes transcend all geographical and cultural barriers, and they occur regardless of time. Understanding their significance not only in mathematics but the occult allows for the lexicon of spiritual understanding, especially when studying more complex patterns such as Metatron's Cube or the Flower of Life.

The first stage of this is the awareness of space or the void. Ginungagap being the primordial abyss that existed before Muspeheim met Niflheim creating the giant Ymir, from whose body the cosmos was created. This empty state is not only the beginning of all geometrical ideas, but it is both the beginning and the end of consciousness. We are born this way, we die this way, and many spiritualists spend their lives attempting to reach this state in their lifetimes. In this sense, nothing is something. The 'thing' remains, despite its cause or effect.

In Christian mythology, this is the concept in Genesis that in the beginning, the earth as without form, it was a void and darkness was upon it. It is the unformed marble, the blank page, the untapped potential. Without this void space, nothing could exist. Many people do not think about a simple dot as a sacred geometrical symbol, but it is. A dot can, like the empty space consciousness, mark a beginning or an end. Think of it like a seed, the point of all creation, all possibilities can emerge from one dot.

Dots inside other symbols can represent the presence of another symbolic meaning, as we see with the Yin-Yang and with many solar symbols like the one with just a circle and a dot in the very middle. Or the solar cross with four dots inside each quadrant of the circle and sixteen dots around the outside. The circle is one of the most prominent symbols in all sacred geometry. Often it is seen as an expanded dot or an unbroken or infinite line. This symbolism is seen in rings, like the myth of the wedding ring. It's seen with the ouroboros and some lore surrounding Jörmungandr as well. A perfect circle has no beginning or end, and its powerful meanings are why it's used so often in ceremonial magic as a protective element.

Hermes Trismegistus explained this as "God is a circle whose center is everywhere and circumference is nowhere." The sun and moon are often depicted as circles, whereas in most spirituality the moon is feminine and the sun is masculine. In most paths in Germanic heathenry, it's the opposite, however. The moon is masculine and the sun is feminine. The circle also has no sides, this is why King Arthur had a round table and the Dalai Lama had a circular council, to symbolize equality.

The vertical and horizontal lines are sometimes thought to represent the same idea, but they're very different. Vertical lines show the vertical axis of Yggdrasil, the ascension of the consciousness from Asgard to Helheim along the World Tree, or vice versa. Horizontal lines have more to do with the material planes and linear time or mankind's path through the world(s). The cross is a mixture of a vertical and horizontal line. In it we see the four cardinal directions or dwarves, the four quadrants when placed inside a circle or square.

The square represents the number four. The four stags that chew Yggdrasil's leaves and the four dwarves. The four major elements that make up the world are also represented with a square. A square has four corners and four sides so a square sometimes may represent the number eight or, more uncommonly, the number sixteen. Eight being the number of legs that Sleipnir has and the number of runes in each of the three ættir in the Elder Futhark. We also know that Odin's name in runes is comprised of four runes, as well as the Hebrew name for their God having four letters.

Next, the triangle is another common symbol both in mathematics and sacred geometry as well as ceremonial magic. It represents the number three as well as any trinity. It can be seen in the symbol of the All-Seeing Eye and pyramids. Triangles are in all four of the elemental symbols from Hellenic civilization. It's the magic triangle of Solomon used in ritual Solomonic magic. Typically, when it's pointed up, it is masculine and down is feminine. In magical terms, pointing up is magic that seeks to unify the practitioner with nature, pointed down is magic that seeks to bend nature to the will of the practitioner.

We see this with the pentagram or pentacle. Various geometrical shapes differ in meaning from each spiritual practice. The pentagram as viewed in a Wiccan practice is much different than how the LaVey or Temple of Set's Nine Angles magical system implements it. Many systems of magic attribute their own meanings to each angle and point within the figure of the pentagram, or they attribute none and use the symbol as a whole, rather than multiple small aspects brought into one piece.

The Valknut

One of the most important figures from a northern European focused practice is the Valknut. Three interlocking triangles making nine points. The modern name Valknútr, meaning "knot of the slain" was given to this symbol seen as early as the 7th century C.E. Often, this symbol is seen being associated with Odin and as we know the significance of the number nine in Northern European mythology, (see chapter on numerology) it stands to reason that this symbolizes those instances in the lore.

Continuing with the geometrical symbols associated with the number nine, we see the Enneagram. The history of the enneagram and the ambiguity of its origin, from medieval philosophers to G.I. Gurdjieff, is detailed in Toby Chappell's book Infernal Geometry and the Left-Hand Path. For the purpose of this book, we will condense the information on the enneagram to this; It is debatable where it originated but we see the idea of a nine-pointed star or symbol across multiple spiritual schools of thought. The geometric symbol representing the Temple of Set's Order of the Trapeziod. The Hindu symbol the Sri Yantra and the Valknut. The Sri Yantra being composed of four triangles pointing up (masculine) and five pointing down (feminine). Like the Valknut, we see three and nine combined with geometrical shapes to create another symbol.

The meaning of the Valknut isn't attested to definitively in the lore and there really isn't any authoritative source on its meaning. However, looking at everything through various lenses is, in part, the purpose of this book. With that said, we can make the philosophical connection between this symbol and the magician (or Erilaz, Eurlian, alchemist, occultist etc.).

We see the number nine deeply imbedded in myths and stories concerning creation and destruction, death and life and representing magical systems pan-cultures. In Christian mythology, Jesus was on the cross until the ninth hour which is also designated as the hour for prayer. There were nine fruits of the spirit and nine spiritual gifts of the holy ghost among other instances that are too numorous to recount concerning the number nine.

In the lore and myths, we see the number nine multiple times as well. There are nine worlds, nine nights that Odin hung, Draupnir reproduces itself every ninth night, Heimdall has nine mothers and there are nine locks on Surt's sword box. Birth, death, creation, destruction. When we look at the Valknut through geometry and numerology, we start to see a bigger esoteric picture. Nine clearly represents a perfect completion. Three, a trinity of creative forces. Knowing the association between Odin and the valknut and knowing the valknut has also been thought for a long time to be associated with death (knot of the fallen/slain).

It's reasonable to come to the conclusion that there might be a magical meaning behind this symbol, or at least represent something to do with magicians. We see the same number of points on the symbol for the Order of the trapezoid, the downward pointing star inside a trapezoid, the bottom point extending past the bottom line of the trapezoid.

The Black Sun

The infamous black sun or the Sonnenrad is an ancient European symbol closely linked to alchemy but rooted deeply in Germanic mysticism and occultism. Sometimes referred to as the sun wheel, the black sun surfaces in a variety of forms with anywhere from four or five to twelve 'rays'. Depending on the number of rays, the meaning changes slightly. Twelve is an interesting number as it can represent the sun's journey through the twelve months in the year or can represent the Gods. We see this with the 12 major Æsir, the twelve Olympian Gods, the twelve Roman Gods, Christ's twelve apostles and so on.

In modern neo-pagan circles, the twelve-ray version of the black sun is often understood as a symbol only prominent in wartime Germany and neo-Nazi hate groups. This is far from the truth, as we see the geometrical and numerological significance within this long-debated symbol (see chapters on geometry and numerology). When talking about the black sun, we cannot ignore the appropriation of this symbol by Heinrich Himmler and the Nazis as the most famous cultural depiction of the Sonnenrad is the mosaic on the floor of Wewelsburg in Germany. There is no evidence to prove who placed the black sun on the floor of that room in Wewelsburg, but the building has ceased renovation.

What we do know is that nothing Nazis used was original to them; Every symbol was taken from earlier Germanic mystics and historians. The Thule Society being one of the more prominent along with practitioners of Armanenschaft, pioneered by Guido von List, another infamous, however when it comes to runes specifically, auspicious character. When studying history, especially one with signs and symbols that have been taken and used for nefarious purposes, it is important to leave emotion out of the quest for knowledge.

While Guido von List had some views that are not accepted as accurate or socially acceptable today, we can glean important esoteric information from his writings and the study of them, especially knowing many of his ideas are the predecessors for many of Himmler's; Though by wartime Nazi Germany standards, Guido von List would have not been tolerated and his books were burned. The alchemical meanings of the black sun are a little different than the generally accepted meaning. Many alchemists use the black sun to symbolize one of the two types of suns. One of these suns being gold and representative of the higher self, the goal of esoteric alchemy and one of the goals of the occultist.

The other being a material and primal sun, or the raw self. The black sun is representative of the latter. Modern pagans associate it, incorrectly, with victory as that is one of the newer associations with the S or Sowilo rune that makes up the rays of the sun. However, more appropriately, in occult terms, it would represent divine victory and higher illumination. The two circles involved in this symbol are another matter to be understood. Circles represent protection and infinity, the number two represents cooperation between two forces. At the very center of the symbol, we see a black hole or dot as well, showing the beginning of everything.

Now we get the bigger picture and why this symbol is important to European mystics. While this symbol, much like the swastika, is often shrouded in controversy, understanding the occult meaning is valuable, whether or not one chooses to implement it in their practice or spiritual journey.

FUNDEMENTALS OF RUNE WORK

Across Europe the original meaning of the word "rune" itself always comes to "mystery" or "secret". The variations of the word from Old Norse, Old English, Old High German, Gothic and even Old Irish and Middle Welsh all define rún, rûn, rûna (for both Old High German and Gothic), rún and rhín respectively as secret/mystery. The Proto-Germanic word rûnô as well means mystery or secret. With Old Norse expanding a bit to include the definitions of written character and magical sign or wisdom. There are other Indo-European words that may be related but are not probable.

When it comes to archeological finds, historical fact that we can tangibly prove, there's not much to go on to prove that runes carried magical weight. While there are a few secret societies that have carried on oral traditions and magical rune knowledge and lore, the public is at a disadvantage when it comes to being able to cite scholarly and historical studies on magical rune work. However, we do have some inscriptions, like the Lindholm amulet that show runes being used for magical purposes. In the case of the Lindholm amulet, it's clear that operative rune work was being used somewhere between 350-570CE.

It was found in the mid 1800s in Sweden and is a carved bone piece that was in a bog, probably put there as an offering to Odin. The inscription begins with the term "Ek Erilaz" meaning "I, the magician" in Proto-Norse and is followed by kennings of the magician including "the wily one", "one of the Sun" and "deceitful one" very reminiscent of Odin's bynames. It then includes a runic formula and concludes with "alu" which is the galdr for Ansuz, Laguz and Uruz which we will cover later.

Another case of an archeological find that shows runes being used for magical purposes is the Kragehul I spear shaft found in the late 1800s and dated between 200 and 475 CE. Its inscription also begins with "Ek Erilaz" and is followed by an inscription that seems to be widely debated. However, their commonality is the beginning. Identifying not only a magical purpose to the inscription in runes but also that it was a title of importance and not a common one. While we don't have much in the way of proof, we have enough to work with on a historical basis. We can go off the Greek magical papyri that originated in Egypt, as that was used in a similar way as runes, using language for magic. However, most will be through the lore. The rest is developing rune work through our study of the lore, through the meanings of the individual runes and through our understanding of magic and the occult.

Runes, while they are a method of divination, are in their own league. While tarot relies solely on the person using the cards, runes have a power they hold on their own and when wielded correctly will bend, break and shape the objective into the subjective will of the magician, Vitki, Erilaz, Rune Worker. All magic works because the magician wills it to work. Things like herbs, wands, candles, incense and other magical tools aid the magician and if used appropriately certainly make any working more powerful; However, without the igniting spark of the magician, they do nothing on their own. This is not the complete case with runes. Much like cooking, if the ingredients are added in the incorrect order, if they're left out or substituted, the recipe can come out wrong or worse, make you sick.

Look at the example found in Egil's Saga. Someone carved runes for healing attempting to aid a sick woman but they incorrectly used them, and it only worsened her condition. Runes, even when not used with ill intent, can cause destruction if the one using them is ignorant or misinformed. Modern examples of misuse of runes can be found just about anywhere. One that was floating around recently was a woman telling others to draw on themselves what she believed to be a bindrune to deflect harmful magic and send it back to the originator. What she drew was Gebo and Tiwaz, essentially marking herself as an offering to the God Tyr. Runes are much like a loaded weapon. When used effectively they can protect you but, if they're used carelessly, they can cause harm to yourself or others. Don't play with weapons, they are not toys.

There are quite a few different futharks (runic alphabets) but the standard for magic and rune work is the Elder Futhark. It was being used in writing between 150-750CE and is considered to be the original runic alphabet. There is validity and power in all the various futharks, but the Elder is what we will use for the purpose of this book when discussing operative rune work. The younger futhark is the most common used in runestones and inscriptions and was used for a longer period of time. Others of note are the Old English Futhorc and the Armanen Futhark. The Old English, sometimes called the Anglo-Saxon Futhorc, isn't commonly used in magic but is seen in archeological findings.

The most debated and either ignored or considered 'bad' is the Armanen Futhark. It should be known about though as all knowledge is important, whether you like the source or not. In world history and even the present time, if we don't know about things that happen, whether bad or good, we can't do anything to condone or condemn them. Furthermore, whether someone was considered to be a good person is irrelevant in this path. We aren't trying to emulate or befriend them. We see evidence almost daily of the horrible things done by politicians and celebrities, at this point it's fairly unavoidable. We know of the Nazi scientists hired by NASA, yet nobody is up in arms about boycotting NASA and still benefit from their work as an organization. So, leaving feelings aside, having a basic knowledge of the Armanen Futhark and its creator is important.

Guido von List, born October 5th, 1848 and died May 7th, 1919, was an occultist and writer, among other things from Austria. List's Armanen Futhark was first published in his book Das Geheimnis der Runen (1908) and seems to be a specific alphabet modified for his magical school of thought. Some of the characters in it, while his 18 runes are said to be an extension of the Younger Futhark, are bindrunes taken from medieval outside sources. It's also intended to be based on the 18 (supposed) runic stanzas of the Rúnaþáttr in the Hávamál (stanzas 138-165). So, while the characters in it are a mixture of valid, ancient letters, it's not a futhark used commonly outside of List's works and there's no need to discuss it or List in much more detail for the purposes of this book.

In a more magical approach, runes are stave figures that correspond to a number, exoteric meaning and esoteric meaning. They each have their own name and phonetic correspondence which leads to galdr. Galdr being akin to a magical chant which can consist of the sound of one or more runes. They also each have their own rune poems or rhymes as well. Deeper than that, they will feel different spiritually and their meanings will change depending on the type of questions asked in casting, carving or pulling. However, their fundamental meanings do not change, and deeper meanings based on the rune poems and rhymes will result in not many variations of understanding.

As stated before, from here out when speaking on runes, we will be referencing only the Elder Futhark. In the Elder Futhark, there are a total of 24 runes, divided into three groups of eight called ættir (plural). The first ætt (singular group of eight), is Freya's ætt. The second is debated and some will call it the Hagalaz ætt, some call it Thor's ætt, Hel's ætt, the Norns' ætt. The third ætt is widely considered to be Tyr's ætt. It doesn't much matter what deity or deities you assign to the ættir though. Some people will just name each ætt by the beginning rune and some don't name them at all. For this book, we will refer to them as first, second and third.

When it comes to the relationships and connections between runes, there are two types of relationship, structural and contextual. Structural relationships are connections made between rune placement in the futhark. This is why their order is important and they should be kept in order. The structural relationship is not always linear, however. When they're arranged in a circle, Fehu to Othala, the runes that sit at various angles are just as useful to each other as runes that sit directly next to each other. This is where geometry and numerology begin to emerge in rune work. The other type of relationship is contextual, when the meanings of runes relate to each other in various ways.

This can be exoterically or esoterically. This relationship will be useful later on in creating bindrunes and runic inscriptions. One example is Isa and Hagalaz. Ice and Hail are related on an exoteric level. However, looking deeper at their secondary meanings, we can see differences and similarities between them. In working with the runes, it's of great importance to remember Hávamál stanza 145 as it can be understood as a warning not just for prayers and offerings but also asking for answers and information from runes. In The Poetic Edda it reads:

> *"Tis better unasked than offered overmuch;*
> *For ay doth a gift look for gain"*

There are multiple translations of the Eddas and the lore and I encourage readers to study each of them and compare and contrast the different versions. Eventually, you'll decide which translation works the best for you. When keeping this quote in mind, it's important to not treat the runes like they're a magic 8-ball. They shouldn't be used to ask questions that are easily found out yourself or things that are irrelevant or unimportant. For example, an inappropriate question would be "Should I wear jeans or a dress today?" or "What's the cheat code to the video game I'm playing?"

That would be the equivalent of using a chainsaw to cut your steak on your plate. It's overkill and with runes, it's unreasonable. Therefore, it's better not to ask at all than to ask too much because as with anything in magic, you have to give something to get something. The runes are no different in that aspect. Granted, offerings to deities require giving more but the same rule applies, just on differing scales.

So, while the runes are powerful and can absolutely change your life circumstances, the lives of others, give information to the magician and much more, they shouldn't be used carelessly and they should first be studied in depth before they're used. To understand anything requires long term study and should be approached from every angle when doing so. With the runes, learning everything you can about them and applying daily study and meditation will aid you in learning and truly understanding them in a faster, more concrete and more whole way than simply being able to list them and draw them.

Following will be a basic explanation of the runes. It should be noted that there are three poems associated with almost every rune. The Old English Rune Poem, the Old Norse Rune Rhyme and the Old Icelandic Rune Poem. Keep in mind, these three vary semi-often as they're all from different cultural and magical backgrounds. It's also important to note that Old Icelandic translation is much more difficult than Old Norse or Old English for multiple reasons. Old Icelandic magic also has its roots in Kabbalah so it's Abrahamic in nature and thus very different from the rest at times, though sometimes the meanings of these poems do agree.

Included in the information about each rune will be the rune name and pronunciation as well as its phonetic sound. Also included will be its placement in the Elder Futhark, which element is associated with it as well as any associations with deities. After that, the exoteric meaning will be given and the contextual information about the rune. To the experienced rune worker, any of the contextual information may be implied in the divination and magical meanings.

As you progress in understanding the runes, the magical and divination implications will expand for you in your readings and castings. For example, a novice rune worker may pull Fehu and think either wealth or poverty. A more experienced rune worker could, depending on the question asked, conclude the Vanir, Freya, Frey or as a warning of some destructive energy at play. Then, magical usage will be for any rituals and offerings you may do in the future and how that rune can aid in those.

Pronunciation: FAY-hu
Phonetic Sound: F
Placement: 1st rune, 1st ætt.
Element: Fire
Deity/Entity Association: Frey and Freya
Exoteric Meaning: Cattle, wealth

Context

To our ancestors, wealth was counted in cattle. It was what fed your family and had the ability to bring more wealth in and what could be sacrificed to the Gods. This is the kind of wealth that is mobile and when cared for with attention and concern, like cattle, will produce more wealth. Just as when money is invested wisely, spent on growth and love, your surroundings will become more stable and prosperous.

This wealth, when hoarded or uncared for, causes destruction, greed and strife. This can also be thought of in terms of spiritual or physical wealth or abundance. Fertility, power, knowledge and wisdom are all forms of wealth to various people. Fehu is also the origin for the English word "fee". Fehu being associated with fire, Freya and Frey brings in sexual energy. As we know, Freya and Frey have much to do with fertility. Fire is often associated with sexual energy and passion.

We often refer to things as "hot" or "steamy" and use fire as a metaphor for attraction and sex. We see in the lore warnings of wealth causing problems when misused. With Sigfried and Fafnir and again with Gulveig, whom many believe to be Freya. These types of warnings about wealth in stories force us to think about whether it is the gold/wealth that is inherently the issue, or if it is humanity's tendency for obsession with wealth that is dangerous. For this reason, Fehu can be productive or destructive. Musspelheim's fire helped create Midgard but the fire during Ragnarok will destroy it.

Magical Usage

Fehu could be used in any magical working concerning wealth, fertility, wisdom, gaining psychic or magical abilities or in a working that will produce wealth. For example, with help to finish a degree or save money to buy a home. It can also be used in magical workings for hexing or cursing someone's finances, descendants or causing infertility.

Divination

When pulled or cast next to runes that imply a favorable outcome, expect wealth or a new opportunity. When next to runes that imply an unfavorable outcome, greed, poverty, discord, infertility.

Pronunciation: OO-rooz
Phonetic Sound: u
Placement: 2nd rune, 1st ætt.
Element: Water
Deity/Entity Association: Buri, Ymir
Exoteric Meaning: Aurochs

Context

The aurochs is a European wild cow that went extinct in 1627. It could grow to be about six feet tall and weigh up to 3000lbs. Like the woolly mammoth, people essentially hunted them out of existence. They didn't produce nearly as much milk as the modern Holstein cow, and they were very much untamable and unmanagble. Uruz represents a vital strength. When it's used with control or used to defend the physical or spiritual self, it can be extremely powerful. Uruz is the force of formation, like Auðumbla, the cow who licks Buri free by licking the icy rime, it's the shaping of a creation.

All the rune poems agree this is something wild that has the ability to create or destroy, much like we see with Fehu. However, Uruz would represent the force or the act of Auðumbla licking Buri free and Fehu would be Auðumbla. It's the will to form something, the catalyst for manifestation and physical creation. It removes the unneeded to shape the creation. When used correctly it is wild, vital forceful energy. In the shape of the stave, we see the 'horns' pointing down toward the Earth whereas Fehu's point up to the sky. Uruz would be the force behind Fehu. The manifestation of creation as Fehu is the substance. Here we see the change between the domestic cattle and the wild Aurochs.

Magical Usage

Uruz acts to amplify other runes no matter the meanings of them.

Divination

When pulled, be aware that determination and willpower are needed. When other runes imply a favorable outcome, it would imply strength, forceful creative energy and good luck. When the reading is unfavorable, weakness and obsession may be at play. Destruction could be implied.

One factor that should be discussed is the extremely varied translations of the rune poems associated with Uruz. The Old Icelandic word "Ur" is difficult to translate. In Sweden and Iceland today, the meaning implies old, primordial or ancient. For example, in Sweden, Urmother means Grandmother.

Looking at Iceland geographically and historically, drizzle or light rain doesn't necessarily fit in with the rest of the information about Uruz from the Old Icelandic rune poem. The process of icy rime melting does however when we go back to the story of Auðumbla licking Buri out. As we see the action of unfreezing or freeing that the poem seems to be talking about. Rime is not the same as regular glazed ice, it's frozen water vapor or frozen fog. Icy rime melting can carve rock and destroy crops whereas a light rain or drizzle, as some translations will use in place of "Ur" for the Icelandic rune poem, doesn't do that type of damage.

Northern Iceland is full of glaciers and stone structures carved from glaciers. Just as the Grand Canyon in the United States, the act of water carving through rock can be an incredible force. Water carving through rock (icy rime melting) fits much better with the rest of the poem and the rest of the information about Uruz we get from other sources as well as the other poems.

In the Gylfaginning (The Deluding of Gylfi) we see another connection to icy rime. We see the connection made between rime giant and frost giant, but we don't see the same interchange between ice giant and rime giant. Often in the older sources we see the connection made between venom and yeast to icy rime. We know now this is water vapor freezing and not venom or yeast. This may be due to the fact that rime's color is not the same as regular ice. Rime is white and ice is clear.

THURISAZ

Pronunciation: THUR-ee-sahz
Phonetic Sound: th or ð
Placement: 3rd rune, 1st ætt
Element: Fire
Deity/Entity Association: Thurses, Thor, Thorn
Exoteric Meaning: Giant, Thorn

Context

Thurses are elemental beings, a race of giants that represent chaos and destruction. While the Æsir are also giants, they are not in the same family as thurses, just the same race. Thurisaz is also called 'the thorn of Thor'. Sometimes associated with Mjolnir, more accurately Thurisaz is the thorn of Thor because it is it the pain or problem for Thor. This rune, while thought to be a protective rune, is not so. Defense is not synonymous with protection for the context of rune work. This is the same kind of defense that a nuclear weapon would be for the one who holds the detonator. It's a directed, destructive force that is defensive as an offensive. So, while you could connect Thurisaz to the thorns on a flower as protection, it is much more directed than that. Destroying something that could cause harm to the magician/erilaz is the only real positive way to view Thurisaz.

Magical Usage

In the lore, we only see Thurisaz used in cursing. In Skirnirsmal or the Wooing of Gerd, we see it said "a thurs rune for thee, and three more I scratch: lechery, loathing and lust". This can either be three Thurisaz runes representative of three curses based on different meanings of Thurisaz or three Thurisaz runes plus three other runes, believed to be either three Laguz runes or three Isa runes. Three Laguz runes make the most sense since the three curses or threats are more hidden and this works with the meaning of Laguz.

There is no doubt based on the words used in the Codex Reguis that at the very least, three Thurisaz runes are used either way. So, we see Thurisaz being used three times with three destructive intentions. The three destructive intentions are understood as starvation and disease, homelessness and nonconsensual sexual contact or rape. So, we see the harnessing of external forces to be directed at the subject as opposed to internal forces being conjured or used for self-purposes.

Divination

When Thurisaz is pulled, this can be a warning to defend yourself or your family or be representative of a negative force or curse coming your way. It's important to notice the runes around Thurisaz and their meanings to divine where this energy is coming from. This could also represent the God Thor or a large problem or stumbling block that is in or is soon to be in your path.

ANSUZ

Pronunciation: AHN-sooz
Phonetic Sound: A
Placement: 4th rune, 1st ætt
Element: Air
Deity/Entity Association: Odin
Exoteric Meaning: A God (Odin), mouth, mouth of God

Context

This represents the wisdom and communication of the God Odin. We see in the lore and the Havamal, the importance of words both in communication with man as well as manifestation. Words are spells and we see them being used as either a conduit for communication or a means to cause harm. Havamal stanza 80, in part, states "it is wise to not waste words". Words are powerful and should not be used in vain. This is also about communication through spoken word of the objective and subjective. So, communicating power through the manifestation of material things.

Magical Usage

Ansuz can mean songs, poems, incantations or spells. Galdr is an important meaning as well as Galdr is the speaking of runes in magic. Ansuz can be used in any magical working to communicate, whether that be with ancestors, spirits or deities. It also comes into play with daily affirmations and mantras. Ansuz's power is why our ancestors regarded spoken word with such reverence and why at one point in time bards were outlawed from singing love songs for fear it would enchant people's wives. We see this in modern times with singers or musicians having huge followings of "groupies" because of hyper-sexual language used in songs about love and sex.

Divination

When pulled in a way that implies a positive outcome, this could mean intellectual achievements, ecstatic experiences, good or favorable communication in the near future or using conversation to gain knowledge. When pulled with runes that imply a negative outcome, expecting miscommunication or stubbornness involving words or a misunderstanding.

RAIDHO

Pronunciation: Rah-EED-ho
Phonetic Sound: R
Placement: 5th rune, 1st ætt
Element: Fire & Air
Deity/Entity Association: Thor, Odin, Norns
Exoteric Meaning: Chariot (Ride)

Context

Raidho is about equal and rhythmic action. You can see this rune in the first and third of Newton's Laws of Motion. Those are that a body in motion stays in motion and a body at rest stays at rest unless force is applied. The other being that for every action, there is an equal and opposite reaction, respectively. The psycho-spiritual wheels are how any journey is made in an esoteric context. Exoterically this is the body or shell. The chariot in which the soul is transported. Whether this journey is a physical or metaphysical one, the journey is often long, slow and can be treacherous.

Magical Usage

Raidho is the vehicle in which 'ek erilaz' comes into existence thus, it is not just a physical transportation. In trance and meditation, the journeying between realms, Raidho is the means to get anywhere. Similar to how the Gods use chariots to traverse the worlds. It is not just forward motion and can be used in necromancy and trace work.

Divination

This almost always implies change. Sometimes a journey and sometimes a change in physicality or geographical residence. When in a negative outcome, it could mean unpreparedness or a hard road ahead.

KENAZ

Pronunciation: KEN-ahz
Phonetic Sound: k
Placement: 6th rune, 1st ætt
Element: Fire
Deity/Entity Association: Frey and Freya, Heimdall
Exoteric Meaning: Torch

Context

Kenaz is the rune of creative forces that shape. This is done through a process similar to the controlled burning used to burn away parts of the forest to make room for new growth or through the fire of the hearth that shapes emotionally through joyful gathering of family and friends. A torch can light your way, ward off potential threats, signal safety or warning.

Fire also carries sexual energy thus Frey and Freya are brought into the meaning of Kenaz at times. Kenaz can also be seen as enlightenment and the torch of knowledge. Kenaz transforms and regenerates, thus symbolizing controlled energy and power being channeled.

Magical Usage

Kenaz is the purifying flame that cleanses a ritual space or sometimes a vé. It drives away harmful energies and can help to shed light on issues needing to be understood or evaluated. It can also be used in sex magic (carnal magic/alchemy), especially when used alongside Nauthiz and Ehwaz and possibly Ingwaz if fertility is part of the intention.

Divination

When pulled in a way that implies a positive outcome, Kenaz can imply creativity or the ability or need for art. It could imply a sexual relationship or transformation as well. When pulled in a way that implies a negative outcome, this could mean sickness or physical debilitation.

GEBO

Pronunciation: GHEB-o
Phonetic Sound: G
Placement: 7th rune, 1st ætt
Element: Air
Deity/Entity Association: Odin
Exoteric Meaning: Gift

Context

The biggest message Gebo gives us is sacrifice. As we see in the lore and especially in the Havamal, returning gift for gift is extremely important. There were even laws in place to penalize those who did not show hospitality. Tacitus writes about this in Germania. This is not only important in mortal relationships but with deities as well. Gods and Goddesses require a sacrifice (gift) with any petition made by a devotee. Nothing is free for anyone. This applies to a more negative aspect as well, eye for an eye. Gebo is representative of equal exchange and the adage "you get what you give" should be remembered when using or studying Gebo.

Magical Usage

Gebo can be used in any working that is aimed at reciprocity. Asking deities or spirits for assistance, linking intentions and energies or to mark something as sacrificial. Gebo is another rune often used in sex or carnal magic during physical and energetic exchanges.

Divination

Gebo, when implying positive outcomes, can mean generosity and exchange. Positive personal reviews from others can be implied as well. If negative, greed and poverty could be expected. This could also represent charity and nonprofit organizations.

WUNJO

Pronunciation: WOON-yo
Phonetic Sound: W
Placement: 8th rune, 1st ætt
Element: Air
Deity/Entity Association: Odin, Frigga
Exoteric Meaning: Joy

Context

Joy is a pretty straightforward definition. Whether it means joy attained from the love one has for spiritual practices and runes, for cooking or any other actions that benefit the self or those around the self. Wunjo is very much about social happiness. The joy one gets from relationships. This can be social or domestic joy brought from romantic, platonic or familial relationships. Harmonious actions where all aspects of the surroundings work with each other for the greater good is another aspect. We see this in kindreds or tribes where the "it takes a village" mindset is implemented in many daily activities.

Magical Usage

Wunjo can be used with any working that is intended to bring happiness and joy. This can be anything from financial help to love workings or justice when used with Tiwaz. On a darker note, Wunjo can be used in hexes and curses when paired with Hagalaz and Thurisaz if the target of the curse's downfall would bring the practitioner true joy or bliss.

Divination

Wunjo being pulled in a positive way implies happiness, harmony and joy. Prosperity and bliss are suggested. When pulled in a negative way, sorrow and strife can be implied. Change for the worse or the possibility of social alienation could happen in the future.

HAGALAZ

Pronunciation: HA-ga-lahz
Phonetic Sound: H
Placement: 9th rune, First of the 2ndætt
Element: Water (ice)
Deity/Entity Association: Hel
Exoteric Meaning: Hail

Context

Hail is a natural destructive force. It destroys fields and homes and can be seen as the solidified wrath of Uruz. The rune poems refer to hagalaz as grain or a seed for the growth of a new formation. Hagalaz is the ninth rune and as the numerological significance of nine being completion, it can be used as a way to bring forth a complete being or energy. Along this line of thought, introspection and this self-awareness resulting from that can be thought of as a meaning of Hagalaz.

Hagalaz works destructively but can be used to destroy something that will lead to something better. When you demolish a rotting house, you can rebuild a home that's sturdy and safe. In essense, hagalaz can be a rune of crisis and misfortune but it can also be the beginning of something much better. Break or dissolve the old to build and coagulate the new.

Magical Usage

Hagalaz works well in cursing or hexing. It can cause a multitude of issues for the target and can be used to regularly rain hail on the target's life. It can cause confusion, loss of property and finances or the ability to have well-tended cattle with Fehu that create regenerative wealth. It can also be used to complete other runes and bring them into a more whole usage. Hagalaz is a powerful force that can move objects and bend seemingly large obstacles to the will of the practitioner.

DIVINATION

Crisis is coming. This may end up as the removal of the dross to make way for bigger and better things or it could be catastrophic. Make sure you are prepared for any possibility when you receive hagalaz as a warning. Do not be caught off guard. Do your best to have the ability to control the crisis so it does not devastate you.

NAUTHIZ

Pronunciation: NOW-theez
Phonetic Sound: N
Placement: 10th rune, 2nd ætt
Element: Fire
Deity/Entity Association: Norns, Hel, Odin, Freya
Exoteric Meaning: Need, need-fire.

CONTEXT

This rune is very much about things that are outside the control of the practitioner. It is about the naturally occurring reaction to actions. In the Old Norse Rune Rhyme, it states "need leaves little choice, the naked man is chilled by frost." Nauthiz also shows that through adversity and distressful situations, a person can become tougher and hardened and better able to handle unpleasant circumstances in the future. Nauthiz can be used to counter fate as well when used as a protective charm. This action and reaction is something we see in ørlög, which is similar to personal, changeable fate. The consequences for your actions, somewhat similar to karma.

MAGICAL USAGE

Nauthiz can be used in "return to sender" workings as a banishing agent. It can also be used to add necessity to other workings and as a runic symbolization of the will of the practitioner. Nauthiz is the "so mote it be" or "my will be done" for runes.

DIVINATION

Nauthiz can imply the need for or the need to lessen self-reliance. Knowing when to ask for support is important for any aspect of life, magical or mundane. However, be sure not to rely too heavily on those around you, do not lose your freedom. Resistance that leads to the strengthening of the familial or social unit can be implied as well.

ISA

Pronunciation: EE-sa
Phonetic Sound: I
Placement: 11th rune, 2nd ætt
Element: Water (ice)
Deity/Entity Association: Skadi, Frey, Norns
Exoteric Meaning: Ice

CONTEXT

Water is fluid while ice is stationary. We see the progression of this element from Uruz to Isa and differing degrees with Hagalaz and Laguz. Ice isn't always destructive and detrimental, but it can be a bridge as well. We see in Havamal stanza 81:

> "At evening praise the day, a torch when it burns
> A sword when tested, a maiden when married,
> Ice when you've crossed it, ale when it's drunk."

Ice, while hard and at times dangerous, can be a bonding agent. As ice is one of two primal forces that met in the Ginungagap, it is just as much of a balancing element as a hindrance.

MAGICAL USAGE

Not only can Isa be used in trance or meditation to metaphysically cross bridges between states of consciousness, but it can be used to block out unwanted energies as well. Isa, as it is a hard material and the stave is a single vertical line, it can also be used in tandem with Ingwaz for fertility working and sex magic. Isa can also be used as a conduit for the ego and ego-consciousness. It can be used in bindings to freeze energies as well.

DIVINATION

Isa in a reading could indicate stasis or the freezing of various matters. This isn't necessarily a permanent fixture, however. It could also imply that a difficult situation is ahead or currently happening that can be resolved through self-control and transitions or unification of various aspects of the soul complex.

JERA

Pronunciation: YARE-a
Phonetic Sound:
Placement: 12th rune, 2nd ætt
Element: Earth
Deity/Entity Association: Frey
Exoteric Meaning: Year

CONTEXT

Jera is the result of the year's labor resulting in a bountiful harvest. The yearly natural cycle ends in the harvest of Jera and if done well, its profits will last the winter. This is the fertility of the land and of mankind. We see Jera used for the celebration for Charming the Plow, which includes a blot to Frey. We also see it used during Winter Nights which is generally around the Celtic holiday of Samhain and the culmination of the year during Yule feast. Jera is about return, the fruits of one's labor.

Magical Usage

Jera can be used in workings for psychological or magical growth, planting seeds of knowledge in hopes of reaping a great accomplishment. It can be used in healing as well to encourage correct energetic flow. It can be used in the same way in mediation. Jera can be drawn or carved into or near anything intended to grow or as a charm to assist right action in natural materials. Jera can be used with other runes to assist in their manifestation or growth.

Divination

Jera almost always is a good omen. Reward, bounty and a good year can be expected. It can also signify a time or place if pulled in a way that requires a measure of time. Negative aspects of Jera could mean that timing for certain things may be off or may conflict with other aspects of life.

EIHWAZ

Pronunciation: AY-wahz
Phonetic Sound: E, I, EI
Placement: 13th rune, 2nd ætt
Element: Air
Deity/Entity Association: Odin, Skadi, Ullr
Exoteric Meaning: Yew

Context

The yew tree is an evergreen tree with red berries. To the pre-Christian Druids, it represented everlasting life and rebirth as well as death and resurrection for the Celts. In this context, Eihwaz represents Yggdrasil, the world tree. We see in Grímnismál that Odin says the god Ullr, stepson of Thor, lives in Ydalir, the yew tree dale. Furthermore, evergreen trees live an extremely long time, which is why they're considered to be representative of eternal life and are often planted in graveyards.

If we think of the yew as a representation of Yggdrasil and Yggdrasil as a representation of man's consciousness and the column with which all things ascend and descend, Eihwaz is a runic representation of the transition from lower consciousness to higher consciousness. Yew is also a great wood for making bows as it is extremely flexible, and we see this imagery with the god Ullr again.

Magical Usage

Eihwaz can be used as a conduit to raise or change consciousness, traverse states of consciousness or worlds and as a link to the material world through grounding. It is the path for astral travel that the chariot (Raidho) takes. When used in the same way as a bow, it can be a way to protect or used as an offensive weapon.

Divination

Spiritual enlightenment and flexibility are often indicated when Eihwaz is read. Movement in the spiritual world is implied or danger that can be transformed can also be an interpretation. Weakness or impairment can be in the negative interpterion of Eihwaz as well.

PERTHRO

Pronunciation: PER-thro
Phonetic Sound: P
Placement: 14th rune, 2nd ætt
Element: Air
Deity/Entity Association: Frigga, the Norns,
Exoteric Meaning: Lot Box or Cup

Context

In games, Perthro is the cup from which the pieces are cast. Interestingly, in the Younger Futhark, Berkano represents both the "b" and "p" sounds and Perthro when looking at the stave, is Berkano opened up or expanded. Gambling, according to Tacitus was of extreme social importance to the Germanic peoples thus, Perthro being the lot box, represents chance or fate.

Perthro is a feminine rune and can represent a female practitioner that deals with divination, wyrd and fate. It is the womb or well from which all things emerge. As it has so much to do with fate and femininity, the Norns and Frigga are implied.

Magical Usage

Perthro representing the womb can be used in both fertility workings and in curses that influence female anatomy. Perthro can represent something hidden or not yet visible in the material world or the psyche and can be used as a way to physically or metaphysically open things up so that they may be visible.

When used this way, Laguz works well with it, allowing more flow. It can point up or down for various needs having to do with pregnancy, unwanted or not. Pointing it down would flush contents out, up would hold things in. When used to influence fate, it can speed things up or slow them down depending on the context and other runes.

Divination

Uncertainty and unexpectedness are implied often with Perthro. It can also indicate pregnancy or fertility. It can be used to understand hidden things having to do with fate and wyrd. Evolution and knowledge are needed.

ELHAZ

Pronunciation: EL-hazh
Phonetic Sound: Z
Placement: 15th rune, 2nd ætt
Element: Air, Fire
Deity/Entity Association: Thor, Heimdall
Exoteric Meaning: Elk, protection

CONTEXT

Elhaz is another rune that has a dual meaning. In Old English, a sword was called "elk-sedge", and we see that Elhaz is used for protection and serves as a warning of danger. It represents the fylgia and higher consciousness as well as connection to the Gods. During blot, we stand in Elhaz position where our bodies mirror the rune stave, this allows our bodies to serve as the link between the Gods and us. This idea is how the Rainbow Bridge (Bifröst) works to connect Midgard to Asgard and where we see the connection to Heimdall.

MAGICAL USAGE

Elhaz can be used to communicate with the Gods, obtain God/Odian consciousness or as a charm for protection. It can be drawn or carved on just about anything for protection. Used in conjunction with Raidho, it can be used as a protective element in astral travel, mediation or physical traveling by plane, train, car or walking etc.

DIVINATION

Elhaz being pulled can represent a protective element or symbolizing a connection with the Gods or higher states of consciousness. It can also warn of danger and selfishness, wrath of the Gods or success in an endeavor.

Sowilo

Pronunciation: So-WEE-lo
Phonetic Sound: S
Placement: 16th rune, 2nd ætt
Element: Fire
Deity/Entity Association: Thor, Baldr
Exoteric Meaning: Sun

Context

Sowilo indicates higher enlightenment, the end result of obtaining Odian consciousness. It is what is hoped for by every practitioner, the light. It's the light that illuminates everything and banishes evil or harmful energy and acts as a shield when made into a sun wheel. Illumination and movement are the main aspects involved. It is the opposite of darkness, but neither can exist without the other.

Magical Usage

Sowilo often represents the use of council from elders or those more experienced or further along in their path. It strengthens the will and can be used with Nauthiz as a more aggressive force of the practitioner's will in magical workings. Its sun and movement are the counter to Isa and can be used to move past spiritual or psychological blockages. Sowilo is the internal victory as opposed to Tiwaz's external victory. Sowilo is the subjective, Tiwaz is the objective. It can also be used to reinforce other runes with solar energy and nature's strength.

Divination

When Sowilo is read, it can indicate hope and successful endeavors. Victory and honor are generally implied. When in a negative light, Sowilo can imply loss and unsuccessfulness. Dishonor and negative influences from those in charge.

TIWAZ

Pronunciation: TEE-wahz
Phonetic Sound: T
Placement: 17th rune, first rune of the 3rd ætt
Element: Air
Deity/Entity Association: Tyr
Exoteric Meaning: Tyr

CONTEXT

In the Old English rune poem, we see Tyr (Tir) described as a dependable star. This is widely considered to be the polestar that acts as a guide for travelers. Tiwaz represents physical and cosmic law and order. Sacrifice for the greater good is implied as Tyr sacrificed his hand to the wolf Fenrir. Tyr is also the original sky-Father or sky God. We see in Gylfaginning that Tyr is described as bold and courageous and a god that the brave invoke.

Tyr is often used to denote someone great in various aspects, the Gylfaginning explains as Tyr-valiant and Tyr-wise. Tyr can be associated with Mars as they are both Gods of war and Tyr is often invoked in matters of justice. Tyr is the God of the AllThing, as he is the God of oaths and honor. However, this is divine justice and not necessarily the justice thought to be fair and right by the practitioner, as this is not subjective justice. For those matters it would be wise to call on Forsetti.

MAGICAL USAGE

Tiwaz can be used in legal matters if the one using it is certain they're in the right. Tiwaz is the rune of stability and sacrifice. It can be used when strength and courage are needed.

DIVINATION

Tiwaz can imply troth and honor. Courage and sacrifice. It can also imply injustice or unjustifiable influences.

BERKANO

Pronunciation: BER-kah-no
Phonetic Sound: B
Placement: 18th rune, 3rd ætt
Element: Earth
Deity/Entity Association: Frigga, Freya, Hel
Exoteric Meaning: Birch

Context

Berkano is the rune of a Goddess. There is disagreement as to which Goddess Berkano represents. For the Tuetonic people, it could be Nerthus and along that same line, Jörd the mother of Thor. Freya is also associated with birch and Berchta is another Goddess tied to birch and has a lot to do with mothers and children. Frigga being associated with the hearth and home, motherhood and childbirth is another associated Goddess. Therefore, it makes sense to recognize Berkano as a representation of Goddesses in general and femininity.

Many traditions had young women dress in birch and flowers for May Day, much like the spring tradition of Nerthus spreading fertility by cart, renewed at the end of this procession with human sacrifice. Birch was often used to symbolize fertility when placed in homes and barns as well. Birch as a method of concealment and protection from outside forces is linked not only to the womb but the burial mound as well.

Magical Usage

Fertility workings as well as any magical work involving a female, whether that be deity or mortal. Any magic that has to do with birth, rebirth or a being coming into power or life, Berkano would be used. When working with disir (female ancestors) and during Winter Nights, Berkano can be a powerful rune to use. Health, glamor or beauty work and love magic also involves Berkano.

Divination

When Berkano is in a reading, it can imply a female influence, often a mother or motherly figure. It can signify a Goddess as well as a female spirit as well. It often means something new is coming into fruition or being born. Negatively, it can mean sterility and stagnant consciousness or lack of growth.

EHWAZ

Pronunciation: EH-wahz
Phonetic Sound: E
Placement: 19th rune, 3rd ætt
Element: Earth
Deity/Entity Association: Frey, Freya, Odin
Exoteric Meaning: Horse

Context

More accurately, Ehwaz is the relationship between horse and rider rather than just the animal horse. Ehwaz is about teamwork and the ability for two separate beings to work together toward a goal or common need/want. It's the relationship between the horse and man, the spirit and body, spouses, friends, and deity and mortal.

This relationship is one generally based on loyalty and respect. Another relation is the fetch or fylgia to the human. The fylgia can be ridden between worlds and operates independently from the rest of the soul complex. It can be used to transmit information between worlds as well or other states of consciousness.

Magical Usage

Ehwaz can be used in any working that means to involve two energies. It can be used in love working or as a way to bend the will of someone else so it works harmoniously with the will of the practitioner. It can be used to either bind or separate depending on the rest of the working and other runes involved.

DIVINATION

Generally, Ehwaz implies some kind of relationship when in a reading, romantic or platonic. Social or as part of a career association. Anyone that works with the reader as a team. It implies, when in a positive light, trust and loyalty as well. Negative meanings can be that someone you work with as part of a relationship means to betray you, there's mistrust brewing or harmony has been interrupted.

MANNAZ

Pronunciation: MAN-naz
Phonetic Sound: M
Placement: 20th rune, 3rd ætt
Element: Air
Deity/Entity Association: Ask and Embla, Odin, Vili and Vé
Exoteric Meaning: Man

CONTEXT

Mannaz is the rune of mankind. Mortal beings of flesh; Humans. It is the rune of human consciousness and that which differentiates mankind from animals. Self-awareness is an important aspect of Mannaz as this sentience is what makes mankind different from the rest of life in Midgard. Mannaz also indicates the whole or fulfilment of the quest of mankind, reaching our potential.

MAGICAL USAGE

Any magical working that means to influence another person or internally assist the practitioner can involve Mannaz. Any working that seeks to gain higher consciousness as a human can be empowered with Mannaz as well. Mannaz works well in matters concerning shadow work and integration of the shadow self.

Divination

When Mannaz is read in a positive way, it can imply any matters concerning intellect, consciousness and the mind. When negative, it can mean blindness and memory issues.

LAGUZ

Pronunciation: LAH-gooz
Phonetic Sound: L
Placement: 21st rune, 3rd ætt
Element: Water
Deity/Entity Association: Njörd, Ran
Exoteric Meaning: Leek or Lake

Context

Water and the ocean have always been viewed as not only a way to gain food and prosperity but a way to travel. It's magnificent and mysterious and both amazement and danger lurk below the surface. Laguz represents the unconscious as well as the fluid portions of the mind and human consciousness like emotion, psycho-spiritual ability and imagination. It represents the space between life and death, consciousness and unconsciousness as well as any journey through water or fluidity.

As Laguz has much to do with hidden or unseen things, emotions and psychic abilities, it is often associated with love as well and two Laguz runes facing each other make Ehwaz. In Sigdrifumál, we see Sigdrifa tell Sigurd to cast a leek in his mead to avoid it being mixed with evil. A similar situation is told in Egil's Saga as well. There are multiple examples of leeks being used to detect poison in the lore as well as old myths.

Magical Usage

Laguz can be used in any working to detect something hidden. Ill-intentions and hidden feelings of others. For those that are experienced in energy working and can pick up on the feelings of others, Laguz can be drawn on the hand and when shaking hands with someone new, their intentions can be easier felt. Laguz can also be used to create energetic flow in any working that involves movement or used as a neutralizing rune in a protective way.

Divination

Laguz generally implies growth, life and journeys. It can also imply something hidden below the surface and fear.

INGWAZ

Pronunciation: ING-wahz
Phonetic Sound: Ing
Placement: 22nd rune, 3rd ætt
Element: Water
Deity/Entity Association: Frey
Exoteric Meaning: Ing (God)

Context

Most believe Ing to be the same as Frey. Ing being a god of fertility, harvest and livestock. This is the rune of gestation, the male version of Berkano. It can also be associated with genetics and the hamingja as it is passed down to a specific heir. Ingwaz is the growing progression of Kennaz to be reaped with Jera.

Magical Usage

Any working that aims to grow something, for something to be reaped later or having to do with vital force can involve Ingwaz. Ingwaz can also be used in any working with fertility or already born children for protection paired with Elhaz.

It can also be used to invoke Frey and is another one we see during Charming the Plow as well as any magic that uses masculine energy. Ingwaz is also a doorway to the astral or metaphysical realms and can be used in lieu of a circle in ceremonial magic as it contains all the aspects of the numerological significance if the number four and the square as well. Other runes can be stored inside Ingwaz as well when creating talismans and magical objects as Ingwaz allows them to gestate and gain power. Using Ingwaz to rob someone of their vitality is another option.

DIVINATION

When Ingwaz is read, one can generally expect internal growing to take place, the subjective aspects of the practitioner are or are in need of growth. Negative meanings could be emotional, spiritual or physical impotence.

DAGAZ

Pronunciation: DAH-gahz
Phonetic Sound: D
Placement: 23rd rune, 3rd ætt
Element: Fire, Air
Deity/Entity Association: Odin
Exoteric Meaning: Day

CONTEXT

Dagaz is about the unification of two opposites. Night and Day. Left and right, masculine and feminine, life and death. It not only represents opposites coming together, but the liminal space between them. The veil, the subconscious, twilight. Polar opposites are brought together to create a new, productive more enlightened consciousness. Synthesis of the mind and body and identifying the greatest of life mysteries, existance as a whole. Dagaz is useful for practitioners involved in working with the dead, spirits and trance. In another sense, it represents the "third eye" being open, the ability to see beyond the material world. It is the rune of ultimate awareness.

Magical Usage

Dagaz can be used to hide things, it is the opposite of Laguz which is used to uncover hidden things. It can also be used with Elhaz when going between worlds and consciousness.

Divination

When Dagaz is read, it can be a representation of consciousness and awakening psychic senses. Awareness of liminal space and the 'in between' is needed or coming. Negative aspects of Dagaz are few. The only negative interpretation of Dagaz could be blindless to spiritual forces and unseen entities.

⊙THALA

Pronunciation: OH-tha-la
Phonetic Sound: O
Placement: 24th rune, 3rd ætt
Element: Earth
Deity/Entity Association: Odin
Exoteric Meaning: Ancestral Property

Context

Othala is the rune for ancestry, kin and homeland. It is the barrier or boundary tht divides the guarded inner halls from the unknown outer halls and beyond. The innangarth and utangarth. It can represent the clan, kindred, tribe or family and the difference between them and strangers. It can be physical property, but also spiritual wisdom and ability that has been passed down in the family or kindred, genetically or socially. While it represents the prosperity and production of the home, order and security are needed for proper usage.

Magical Usage

Othala can be used to invoke Odin or in ancestral work. In meditation it can be used to connect with the spirits of deceased ancestors. Used in a kindred setting, it strengthens the bonds of kinsmen and aids in the passing on of tradition. Any workings involving the home or domestic living place, ancestors and family can involve Othala. It can also be used in matters of legal inheritance, especially when paired with Tiwaz.

Divination

When Othala is in a reading, it implies ancestry, family, home and at times, Odin. It can be family that is physical, blood related or spiritual family. Negative aspects can include dictatorship, homelessness and lack of order.

ALCHEMICAL RUNE WORK

Everything we do can be understood by breaking it down conceptually, looking at the information objectively and forming a subjective individual understanding based on the information we've learned. Therefore, not only understanding the runes, but practical usage of them can be done the same way. Having a few layers of fundamental exoteric knowledge of each rune and its meaning, we can begin to combine or isolate them using the alchemical process.

When we look at each stave individually, we not only see the rune itself, but many times we see other runes as part of each stave. When we look at Jera, for example, we can see two Kenaz runes facing each other staggered. What information we can infer from this can be used to further our understanding of both Jera and Kenaz.

Kenaz is the torch, transformation and enlightenment through purifying flame. Jera is the harvest, the reaping of rewards that have been allowed to grow over time. Doubling runes in runic inscription uses numerological significance and we know that two is symbolic of cooperation between two forces. We could then take Jera to mean the doubling of Kenaz's energy as a transformative and enlightening rune, and from there use it in our practice to assist in matters of spiritual enlightenment for the purpose of transformation.

Even further than that, when used alongside herbs and various products that coincide with this meaning, we can create a more complex magical working. The snake is often a symbol of knowledge and enlightenment and if we use either the animal itself or imagery of it, coupled with Jera as two Kenaz runes, we get a charm or working for intense spiritual enlightenment. Another example in a bit of a different way is Mannaz and Dagaz.

We see that if we extend the bottom lines downward on Dagaz, we get Mannaz. Taking time to reflect on what this might mean brings us a different understanding. With Dagaz being the twilight consciousness or the awakening of psychic senses and Mannaz being mankind and our sentience, it's interesting to see Dagaz inside Mannaz as that's what every magician or occultist seeks to achieve within him or herself. Every rune has multiple layers of esoteric symbolism. When one makes the effort to uncover them, they do not simply need to be an alphabet.

These meanings, when taking geometrical placement and numerology into account, can mean more than just the base exoteric meaning for any rune or combination of runes. As discussed earlier, which way something faces has meaning as well as the number of times it's repeated and the points of contact within a bindrune or sigil. Therefore, when making bindrunes, it's important to check which runes are part of each stave. We do not need to use both Mannaz and Dagaz in a bindrune because the stave of Dagaz is already inside Mannaz.

Dissolving the rune to its most basic forms is another important aspect of understanding. When we look at Hagalaz for example, we see two Isa runes with a bridge between them. Isa is solid, immovable and hard. It can be impossible to pass if one's will seeks to make it so. When we move along Hagalaz from one Isa, we cross a bridge only to be met with another Isa. There we see another layer of Hagalaz that can be used in magical working. Hard, impassable object after hard, impassable object. Relentless struggle. This understanding would aid in using Hagalaz in curses and hexes.

There are other runes which seem to differ very slightly. Take Thurisaz and Wunjo. With Wunjo, if one chooses to view it as Isa with Kennaz facing it at the top, we see a joyous torch, a harbinger of happiness and safety. When we move that Kennaz down to the middle of Isa, as we see with Thurisaz, Kennaz is above and below ice, making the flame pointless. What good is fire when ice surrounds it, enveloping it in hardness and closing off the way to get past it? We then see the torch of inspiration and enlightenment made ineffective. This adds to the treacherous nature of Thurisaz, doubling up the devastation caused by it when using it against someone.

Gebo and Nauthiz differ slightly as well. We see the symmetry of Gebo slightly altered, set askew in Nauthuiz. If we bend that horizontal line back slightly, we see Gebo again. We see intrinsic, human, primal need transformed into reciprocity when given symmetry. This can be understood as basic human nature. When we as mankind receive what we have to have, when our basic needs are met, it sets a natural course of give and take working together. We have our needs met and then are better prepared to care for our surroundings and contribute productively to nature and society as a whole.

When looking at Eihwaz, we see that it is an ambigram but also contains two Laguz staves no matter how you look at it. Laguz being representative of the unconscious and hidden aspects of human psyche and shadow selves, the meaning doubles in Eihwaz as we see the traversing between lower and higher states of consciousness. In either direction, Laguz, the unconscious is linked with the passing between Asgard or higher consciousness and lower consciousness or Midgard and Helheim along Yggdrasil which can be thought of as the entirety of existence for mankind.

Berkano opening up into Perthro was briefly covered in the rune section, but what does this mean esoterically? Berkano is the Goddess rune. In universal occult terms, the divine feminine. Perthro is fate and the womb, the space from which life emerges. We then make the connection not only to reproduction but, spiritual ascension and the passing of spiritual knowledge. We can also see the divine feminine opening up into the womb-space of fate and further down that road, sejd magic. Sejd magic being an almost exclusively feminine magical art.

Each rune can be used to better oneself when studied in depth. When using the runes as a focus in meditation, with or without galdr, you connect the rune to your subconscious. Some argue that the runes are already in the subconscious, passed down by our ancestors, but for those who don't have that or feel called to rune work, studying them deeper is a must. Studying each rune doesn't just include academic research either. One of the best methods for developing the skill of runic thinking is mediating each day for nine days on every rune in order. When doing so, afterward take note of any feelings, colors, numbers and other symbols that come to mind when meditating.

While meditating, it's important to not stray in thought when you're just starting out with runic mediation. Thoughts will come, nobody can think of just one thing when they first start. When you have thoughts while meditating on a rune, accept them and release them and refocus on the rune. Eventually this will become easier and focusing won't be as difficult.

Breaking each rune down to its essential components, shape, sound, name, and meaning and taking time to focus on each aspect is how you understand them. Further than that, noticing how each rune feels, what colors and shapes come to mind and where you notice each rune in your day-to-day life helps you connect with them on a deeper level. Once you know them on an academic level and a spiritual level, you can begin to use them in spell work.

Nine out of the twenty-four runes in the elder futhark are ambigrams. These nine runes are most essential to not only human nature but also critical magical development. Gebo, gift in the form of reciprocity is a naturally occurring process. It is the runic equivalent of 'as above, so below'. Hagalaz, hail is a powerful and destructive force, linked to willpower and the introspection that leads to a new level of self-awareness and understanding. It's what's needed to reach the level of Dagaz by use of Sowilo and Eihwaz. Isa is involved in everyone's lives, mundane or otherwise.

Everyone faces hardship, learning curves and obstacles they must overcome which, if allowed to properly gestate and come to their full potential with Ingwaz, they can be reaped with Jera. This is the process of Nauthiz working with Eihwaz through the occultist to obtain the highest understanding or consciousness. In essence, this is a form of Jungian-inspired shadow work. The process of bringing the unconscious forward to the conscious and knowing oneself as deeply as possible. The shadow being the unconscious part of our psyche. This is where our subconscious urges come from. Trauma, bias, untapped potential and other aspects of our minds lie suppressed and dormant, acting as an invisible force that pushes us to act, speak and think in a certain way.

It's where all of the characteristics we dislike about ourselves lie. Sloth, greed, gluttony, selfishness, anger and hatred all reside in the shadow of the ego. Those things that when left alone, unhealed and unrecognized can become destructive and infectious. It's important to note that not all of the shadow is full of horrible negative aspects. Untapped creativity and abilities one is not yet conscious of also lie in the shadow. Going through this idea and the process of shadow work looks dark and tumultuous but, it's the darkest before the sun rises. Things always get worse before they're better and the first step can be frightful, but it is worth it to get to the other side where the light shines.

The purpose of this is to free yourself of these unseen aspects of your psyche. The ability to understand why you think and act instead of mindlessly doing so untaps a well of spiritual and mental growth. Magically, this is how you make your magic work. You cannot be an occultist or magician that produces fruit without knowing yourself and integrating your shadow. Not only that, but your confidence blooms, weakness will dissipate and it will eliminate magical and mental limitations. The goal is not to be financially successful or conventionally powerful as many think.

Those snake oil salesmen peddling self-help shadow workbooks with the promise of riches are wolves in sheep's clothing. They're liars and charlatans. The goal of shadow work is to free yourself of the instinct of urgency and necessity to obtain those conventional signs of success. To know yourself inside and out and be free of the social and existential fear and anxiety. To shut the expectations of humanity out of our life and instead live within our own self-acknowledged and personal set of law and order.

This process can be used in a multitude of ways. It can be used for personal self-improvement similar to shadow work as a way to become more in touch with yourself as runic shadow work. Another way of utilizing this 9-rune process, which we can refer to as the Erilaz Method, is as a study tool. Taking whatever concept or material you wish to gain more information on or understand at a deeper level, you can put it through this alchemical process and come to a more in depth understanding of the material. The Erilaz Method is a nine-step technique involving the stages of the alchemical process. Each of the ambigram runes symbolizes a step beginning with Nauthiz and ending with Jera.

At the end of this book, there will be pages for the reader to practice the utilization of this method for any subject they desire. From individual runes to personal struggles, the Erilaz Method can help disassemble the components of the issue and reassemble the material in a way that's easier to understand and work with. The best way to do this is to take nine days for each step in the process. This isn't a quick fix, nor should it be used in place of therapy and mental health help when needed. It is simply something one can do to understand themselves or something they desire more fully. You cannot work your will on the objective universe if you cannot work your will on yourself.

Changing yourself for the better is how we accomplish better and can lead better lives. Here we will have a breakdown of the process in an introductory way as the first step of your journey in shadow integration as well as internal alchemy or a study form of academic alchemy. This isn't an exhaustive plan but can serve as a building block for further study and psychological self-work. The most important part of all of this is honesty. If you aren't honest with yourself, who can you ever be honest with? You have to do this work without judging yourself, without censoring yourself and without lying to yourself or it will never work.

Step One
Nauthiz – identification of need

Identifying the need for the process to take place is the first and most important step. Knowing there's a problem is usually half the battle. If the problem is a personal one, such as envy or anger, identifying that one struggles with this is something most refuse to admit. Being able to admit this to yourself is worth acknowledging and being proud of. If the need is an academic one, such as understanding Odin as a deity, you're already further down the road than many who claim to be occultists or witches or whatever label they choose to take on. The world is full of armchair occultists, those who can regurgitate talking points, list the names of books by famous occultists, but can't seem to get a handle on their ego or explain many theological points from a unique individual understanding. They simply do not want to put the work in. If you're choosing to spend the time and energy doing the work, you're leagues ahead already.

Step two
Hagalaz – objective breakdown

In this step, we are mimicking the calcination with traditional alchemy. Putting yourself in the heat, so-to-speak. Without judgment, recognizing weaknesses and through examination of these attributes, we make the unconscious, conscious. Eventually, with recognition and following the next steps, you will no longer be guided on impulse and urges based on unawareness. If you have a proclivity to have thoughts of envy, you're going to use this step to study that thought and the feelings and emotions that trigger it as if it were a detached scenario. You can do this with any weakness you feel you need to address. For nine days, write down every intrusive envious (or any problem) thought in its entirety.

Write it in as much detail as you can as if you're writing a script for the screen. The other people involved, what actions occurred before and after the thought, everything you can write down, do so. For a study area, this is the stage where you'll write down everything you know about the subject. If it's Odin, write down everything you can think of that relates to him that you know, without having to research. Every bit of information you're already aware of. Do this also for nine days.

Step Three
Eihwaz – conversing with the shadow

If you've ever purchased a new pair of shoes or a vehicle, most of us begin to notice that we start seeing it everywhere. All of a sudden, everyone seems to be driving that car or wearing the same shoes as us. Why does this happen? One reason is that we're now looking for it subconsciously. This is, in part, how manifestation works. What you look for is what you'll find. What you choose to take in is what you'll receive. Obviously, this doesn't work in all situations, but in its most basic form, this is the basic mechanic behind manifestation. Making the unconscious, conscious.

The Hagalaz step helps to set this in motion. When you've taken time to notice your weaknesses, your triggers and your responses, you'll start to notice patterns. Go back to your notes and without judgment of yourself, notice the similarities between these situations. Numbers, people, certain language, places, food, weather. Anything that's a recurrence, write it down. With study material, go back and make sure nothing that's written down is an opinion.

Stick with facts. If you aren't sure if something is factual or not, make a note of that. Starting with this step, begin to be mindful of your actions and feelings. When you begin to feel that you're getting upset, angry, envious, lazy or anything else, become aware of it beginning to happen. Starting with this step, also begin a dream journal. Keep it by your bedside and every time you wake up from a dream, write it down in as much detail as possible. Later in this process, we will begin to notice patterns in images, feelings and themes from your dreams.

Step Four
Gebo – exchanging transference for understanding

People say, sometimes in an unkind or arrogant manner, that whatever you dislike in someone else, is part of what you dislike in yourself or lack in your life. While this is a hurtful statement, it is also fairly true. Aside from universal morality issues such as dislike of murderers or liars etc. the aspects that feel repetitive that we dislike tend to have deeper psychological meaning. If we constantly feel the need to insult someone's appearance or status in society, that almost always reflects an insecurity in our own life.

Even when we admire a person, this can turn into a form of mental worship that hinders growth. Look at your notes and recognize themes that relate to runes. What rune or runes can you associate with the repeating themes in the problem scenarios you've been consciously studying? Write down the rune or runes that reflect the issues you've faced and take nine days to study the rune or runes.

In this time, meditate while picturing the rune, write down any thoughts or feelings, numbers and colors, shapes or animals you think of during that time. With study material, you can associate one or more rune(s) with the study material and do the same exercise. The second part of this process is to take the good and discard the rest.

Separate the needed from the unneeded or the pure from the dross. Which aspects of yourself no longer serve your best interest? What do you want to leave? For study, compare what you know to academic proof. What did you get right and what do you need to work on? Take notes on what things you need to focus on more and keep that in mind.

Step Five
Isa – Hardening and Integrating the Shadow

Taking the runes associated with the psychological problem area or the area of study, we can begin the process of conjunction. This is where we recombine the material into something of value. For the process of runic shadow work, this part of the Erilaz Method can take longer for most. Identifying emotional themes and their runic counterparts, we can begin to integrate the shadow. We do this by first finding our archetype. There are 12 Jungian archetypes. The Ruler, Artist, Innocent, Sage, Explorer, Outlaw, Magician, Hero, Lover, Jester, Everyman and Caregiver. Archetypes are symbolic representations that not only do we see in mankind, but in everything created by mankind as well.

Every story has archetypal characters. Myths, fictional entertainment pieces, movies and various other mediums of expression. Once we discover what archetype we are, we can learn to understand ourselves better. Whether or not we deeply believe in the existence of archetypes we see in media, we can gain, to an extent, a basic connection to ourselves and then relate that to the lore and various other myths and legends. Then, we can use that to strengthen mindfulness of our emotional and material behavior. We can also use that to understand others on a deeper level as well. It also gives us a new, more serious view of religion and myths on a psychological level, not necessarily in a literal way. This pushes us down the path that Jung calls individuation. We're referring to it here as spiritual alchemy.

Step Six
Ingwaz – Gestation

We've been journaling our triggers and identifying patterns. We've been taking notes of people we idolize or dislike and what they represent in ourselves that we like or dislike. We've also been working on our dream journals and hopefully noticing patterns in theme, feeling, characters or archetypes in these dreams. At this point, meditation on runes and aspects of ourselves has become a regular occurrence as well. At this stage, we rest. Keep journaling and identify what parts of this process are working well and which ones are harder for you.

Step Seven
Sowilo – the will refined

Now that we've identified what parts of this process are more difficult and have noticed patterns, become more mindful of our behaviors and begun to trace back our weaknesses and strengths to their origins in our life, we can begin to refine our will and use it to make ourselves and our life better. Make a list of goals, some big, some small. Write down all of them, even the ones you feel may be unrealistic. When you write them, do so in a way that says you have already accomplished them and be specific. Make some that are immediate and some that may take some time. Make goals that are various levels of difficulty as well. An example list of goals can look like this:

1. Tomorrow, I will wake up happy and excited for the day.
2. This week I will deep clean my living space.
3. In 30 days, I will have a thousand dollars in my bank account.
4. In less than one year, I will own the house I want.
5. I am free of the need to chase money, but instead it comes to me.
6. I know my body and mind.
7. I can see through manipulation of others.

Whatever goals matter to you, write them down and put them somewhere you will see them often, at least once a day. You do not need to dwell on them throughout the day or chant them. Just read them to yourself at least daily. Every time you read them, say "my will be done" or some form of that sentence as long as it is authoritative and stern. This will allow these goals to become attached to your subconscious and be able to manifest easier. If you believe in magic, words are spells and what you speak is heard by the universe, the Gods and nature.

Step eight
Dagaz – coagulation of day and night

In this step, you will be aware of your shadow and be on the road to integrating it completely. This is a lifelong journey for most and will not be a quick process. The ego is a tool. Just like a hammer, it can be used to build or to destroy. What you choose to do with it is what will manifest. Be ready to repeat this process as many times as needed and sometimes to struggle. Life is a constant struggle for wholeness, and many do not reach the goal of becoming whole in this lifetime.

Integrating your shadow, recognizing weakness and untapping potential for greatness is further than most will ever get on the path to enlightenment, illumination, God or Odian consciousness, whatever term you wish to use for turning yourself into gold. During this step in your journal, be sure to take notes on successful manifestation or spell work and what fails. When you experience a failure, try to associate it with a rune and meditate on that rune for a few days or weeks. Furthermore, trace the feeling you get through your shadow and be mindful of why you feel how you do.

Step nine
Jera – the erilaz and the harvest

Knowing your ego can be used for help or harm, they can be achieved and avoided respectively. Use the knowledge of yourself to understand those around you, to be a more understanding parent, friend, spouse, occultist, magician. Revel a little in your ability without letting your ego control you. Reap the benefits of your work by getting magical results and unlocking deeper mediation and trance. Use what you know to grow yourself and, remembering Fehu, to spread knowledge and assistance.

This process could and should be used throughout your life. Do not become so comfortable or egotistical that you stop working on yourself. One successful working does not make an occultist. Be prepared to ride highs and lows in this journey and be willing to know when to ask for help, seek guidance or delve deeper. Honesty and open-mindedness are the key to shadow work and without them, no successful magic will be produced, and growth cannot be expected.

ALCHEMY IN THE LORE

"Odin the Wanderer" by Georg von Rosen (1886)

Odin is the epitome of an Alchemist, and the lore is filled with alchemical allegories. We see this not only in the aspects of Odin as a deity, but the various stories of his antics and the things he chooses to seek after. Knowledge is of foremost importance to an alchemist and occultist. Interestingly enough, it's also the main attribute or characteristic of many of the typical demons and devils of monotheism, knowledge and light. The snake in the garden of Eden offered Eve to eat from the Tree of Knowledge of Good and Evil. It was knowledge and immortality he offered, the same things alchemists, occultists and Odin seek.

The Big Bang Theory states that the universe began as a single, dense, hot point. A supercharged black hole. It violently exploded, creating matter, space, time and energy. We can reconcile this with many mythological explanations concerning the origin of the universe. Many believe myths to be primitive and their archaic stories to have been explained scientifically, which is often viewed as better. As occultists, we generally believe that science and magic are explaining the same ideas in different languages. Some aspects of life, science is too young to comprehend and therefore, we look to older understandings.

When the fires of Muspelheim met the ice of Niflheim, Ymir was created. Here we see heat and cold coming together in the yawning void, Ginungagap, to create matter, life. This action is repeated in nature infinitely but also in esoteric alchemy. The first step of the alchemical process is the first step in nature, in the Big Bang Theory and in the myth of the creation of the world in Northern Europe. We also should note the numerological significance of one Ginungagap being transformed by two polar energies, Muspelheim and Niflheim and then becoming one again with Ymir.

The beginning is transformed and again begins anew in a different form. Alchemically, the unconscious void, Ginungagap, becomes the conscious hermaphroditic giant, Ymir, thus being an allegory for the Alchemical Marriage. The Alchemical Marriage is a term for the unification of the unconscious and conscious, masculine and feminine, essentially the goal of the occultist and the end result of shadow work.

The other being that emerged from this meeting of fire and ice, was Audhulma, the primordial cow that fed Ymir and licked Buri free from the ice. Thus, without Audhulma, Ymir would not have survived to create giants, one of whom married Buri. Buri, the father of Bor who married Bestla, who gave birth to Odin Vili and Ve. Unlike many ancient myths that result in a trinity of deities, there is no virgin birth. Instead, there's a hermaphroditic giant and a primordial cow. The themes remain similar, however. A trinity including three different purposes for each aspect of said trinity is not an uncommon myth.

We see this in the Egyptian story of the father Osiris, the mother Isis and son Horus. In Mesopotamia, we see the father Nimrod, the Mother Semiramis and the son, Tammuz. In Hindu mythology, we see Brahma the creator, Vishnu the preserver and Shiva the destroyer. The Phoencians had El, Baal or Melqart and Astarte. All of which are believed to be much older than the Christian trinity, though usually symbolizing similar ideas, sans Christian dogma.

After Odin, Vili and Ve killed the giant Ymir, the birth of the objective material universe comes into the lore. A trinity, whether you believe that Vili and Ve are other aspects of Odin or three separate deities, creating the known world. Again, the alchemical idea of breaking something down to create something new is a recurring theme. The slaying of Ymir is one of the most obvious alchemically infused stories in the lore. To humans, the objective world is eternal. It's all we will ever know and see. Odin, Vili and Ve creating this eternal world from the blood and body of Ymir is esoterically the creation of immortality.

In another way, the immortality of Odin, Vili and Ve is beginning to solidify with this story as well. In the Havamal, we are told that the one thing that never dies are the deeds of men. Just the process of writing this and the reader consuming it aids in the immortality of Odin, Vili and Ve as we are thinking of them and learning of them. Nobody truly dies if they're remembered. We've seen the calcination step with Muspelheim and Niflheim resulting in dissolution in the meeting of the two. The third step, separation, is seen with Ymir feeding from Audhulma who licks Buri free. Recombining it into value by Odin, Vili and Ve killing Ymir and creating the material universe, Midgard.

Midgard was allowed to ferment and grow, safe in the protective wall during the fifth step of the alchemimcal process. It was increased in purity during the distillation step with the creation of Ask and Embla from ash and elm wood. The coagulation was the resulting population beginning with Ask and Embla who were given sentience from Odin, Vili and Ve. One of the many similarities between Northern European lore and Christian mythology is the story of Bergelmir. After the killing of Ymir, there was so much blood that all the frost giants were drowned.

Only Bergelmir and his wife managed to survive by escaping on a boat. The story of Noah and his family being able to survive the Christian God flooding the earth is similar and in many of the fundamentalists Christian groups, the belief is that the Biblical flood drowned all the Nephilim who were believed to be giants as well. Most cultures have some kind of myth involving a giant flood, the semi-arguable oldest story being in the Epic of Gilgamesh. The next example of this process can be seen with Mimir's Well and Odin's eye. Odin sought wisdom from the well of the wisest being he knew, Mimir. In return, Odin removed something that he didn't need in order to gain knowledge, or something he felt he did need.

The removal of Odin's eye for knowledge has multiple layers of esoteric truths. Firstly, sacrifice of the flesh for a greater purpose is a long-time occult theme. This type of sacrifice is prevalent in almost every story we know of. Interestingly enough, there's a Muslim belief that the Dajjal, or false messiah, will have one eye. This belief has seeped into some fringe fundamentalist-Protestant Christian sects in modern times as well. The belief being coupled with a translation of Jesus' sermon on the mount in Matthew 6:22-23 and some seemingly obscure ideas surrounding the Jewish Talmud.

It leaves us to wonder if the one-eyed Odin inspired some of the 'evil' characters at play in other religions, which will be covered in another book. It's also interesting to note the similarities between the head of Mimir and the story of the beheading of John the Baptist of Christian mythology. Mimir was beheaded by the Vanir who thought they'd been cheated during the exchange of hostages during their war with the Æsir. John the Baptist was beheaded because he spoke out against the marriage between King Herod and his wife (niece) Herodias. However, both characters were considered exceptionally wise and were both grieved by their leaders. Odin used herbs to preserve the head of Mimir and Jesus grieved. Jesus' followers also sought out John the Baptist's head to give him a proper burial.

Maybe a stretch, but the similar theme is worth noting. To take the alchemical connections to Odin a step further, let's look at Odin through the lens of being a trinity-God along with Vili and Ve. If we think of all three of these deities as one singular deity, Odin, we can uncover even more esoteric alchemical knowledge. When giving life to Ask and Embla, Odin gave them breath of life, Vili gave them consciousness and Ve gave them appearance. All three of these gifts are what makes mankind. "Odin" means master of inspired consciousness. "Vili" means volition or willpower. "Ve" means sacrality; we perform ritual and blot in a sacred enclosure called a ve.

On both levels, these three gifts and meanings of these names are the essentials of humankind, they are what make everything in the manifest world as well. Life, will and sacredness. Here, we can see that we can then make the argument that Odin is connected to, if not the same being, as Hermes Trismegistus. In the second to last line of the Emerald Tablet, "It is for this reason I am called Hermes Trismegistus; for I posess the three essentials of the philosophy of the universe." Thus, this only further pushes the idea that Odin is the epitome of an Alchemist.

In the Prose Edda, we see an example of a fairly common ritual of frith that involves a group, clan or kindred all spitting into a bowl. The Gods and Goddesses do this and create Kvasir. The action of creating something from the blending of essences is not just an occult theme but a natural one as well. Alchemically, this is another example of the alchemical marriage as well as the seven-stage alchemical process condensed. More hints of alchemy are brought about in the ending of Kvasir's life when he is killed by the dwarves Fjalar and Galarr and his blood, mixed with honey, made into the mead of poetry.

The mead was put into two vats called Bodn and Són and a kettle called Ódrerir. The two dwarves proceed to kill a giant named Gillingr and his wife. When the son of the murdered giants, named Suttungr, learns of his parent's demise, he attempts to kill the dwarves and is given the mead of poetry as recompense. Suttungr hides the mead in Hnitbjörg to be guarded by his daughter, Gunnlöd. Odin then went to where nine thralls were cutting hay with their sythes and offers to whet the blades for them. Odin ends up talking up his whetstone so much after the thralls realize how much sharper their sythes are.

Odin throws the whetstone up in the air and when the tralls all try to grab it, they end up killing each other with the sharpened sythes in the process. Odin then proceeds to the giant Baugi, brother of Suttungr, the master of the nine thralls who is lamenting the loss of his workers. Odin, calling himself Bölverkr, then offers to do the work of these nine in exchange for one drink of Suttungr's mead. Baugi explains that he doesn't have control over that, but he would go with Bölverkr/Odin to try and get it from Suttungr. Eventually they get to Suttungr who refuses a drink of the mead, so Bölverkr/Odin suggests to Baugi that they take the mead anyway.

They bore into rock to reach the place where the mead was by use of Rati, the augur. Odin realizes Baugi meant to deceive him, transforms into a snake and reaches the mead and Gunnlöd. Odin lies with Gunnlöd for three nights and she gives him permission to have three droughts of the mead. Odin proceeds to drink all of the mead from all three containers, transforms into an eagle and flies toward Asgard. Suttungr takes the shape of an eagle as well and gives chase to Odin after realizing his mead is all gone. Upon reaching Asgard, Bölverkr/Odin spits the mead out into the vats the other Æsir had waiting.

Once again, we see the theme of the breaking down of a material, this one being Kvasir, to its base level, blood or lifeforce. The base material is then transformed into something of value, this time being mixed with honey and allowed to become mead. Just in the process of creating mead, we see the alchemical process as well. The birth, death and subsequent re-birth of Kvasir is not just the fairly literal alchemical process but the natural life, death, rebirth cycle that occurs in all nature. A seed becomes a tree, becomes a source of food or building material, oxygen, shade. It then dies, falls and feeds the ecosystem where it rots, becoming part of the world around it in a different way. This cycle is in every myth, story, being and natural phenomena we know.

The significance of the number three is evident in every spiritual path, no matter its origins. When Gollveig, believed to be Freya, is burned three times and three times born, as the lore states, when she is the first to come to the Æsir Gods, this begins the Æsir and Vanir war. Freya being the feminine epitome of a magician, alchemist or seeress being killed by fire three times yet coming back from this all three times further shows the evidence of this trifold deity archetype having explicit power, more so than other powerful deities. Gollveig, meaning "gold greedy" or "gold might", being refined and reborn by way of fire is an obvious alchemical story.

As we know, the main goal of the traditional alchemists was to turn base metals into gold by way of fire. Gold is often described as fire or fire as a kenning for gold. As in the Icelandic rune poem, the piece on Fehu or wealth, it is called the fire of the flood tide or the fire of the sea. This also relates to the God Ægir who lights his hall under the sea with gold. Six being a number that represents strength, it makes sense that the chain binding the wolf Fenrir would be made of six 'impossible' things.

A cat's footsteps, the beards of women, the roots of a mountain, the nerves of bears, the breath of a fish, the spittle of a bird. The impossibility of cats being attested to more with the fact that Freya's chariot is driven by cats, something else we know to be fairly impossible. Immortality is, in part, the goal of some alchemists and occultists. This isn't necessarily a physical immortality, however. As mentioned before, nobody ever truly dies as long as they are remembered. However, physical immortality has been the goal of many humans since the dawn of time.

We see this reflected in the lore with Idunn's apples. The Gods are not immortal on their own, they eat the golden apples of immortality when they begin to feel old, which prolongs their life. Apples have always been symbolic of eternal youth and immortality. In Svipdagsmol, Groa's spell has many alchemical ideas as well. In this story, as other stories, it begins with someone reaching out to the land of the dead for help. A man named Svipdag calls for his mother, Groa, to help him even after death. She chants nine spells to help Svipdag. In any story, it's important to remember the numerological significance of the numbers involved.

Here, the number nine and it's meaning along with geometric shapes having the number nine involved, such as the enneagram and Valknut. She does this to protect him from death as he attempts to reach Mengloth in her house of flame, at the behest of his stepmother. Mengloth meaning "necklace-Glad", and again believed to be Freya or possibly Frigga. In the second part of Svipdagsmol, called Fjolsvinnsmol, Svipdag answers questions correctly about the world and those in it and is awarded his bride, Mengloth. A beautiful love story and a wonderful alchemical one. Beginning with the bringing back of the dead for help, protecting oneself with magic in order to travel to a fire palace and win love after this journey. Love being another immortal idea in many belief systems.

THE INFINITE GODS

Many myths and stories are repeated throughout history, across multiple cultures. While the names of deities change, some themes remain. Krishna came a thousand years before Christian mythology and was a shepherd, his father said to be akin to a carpenter and born to a virgin. Persia's Mithra, another pre-Christian God, was born to a virgin, had disciples, was crucified and resurrected on the third day. There's also many similarities between Christian mythology and stories coming out of Egypt with Horus. The Epic of Gilgamesh, an epic style poem from Mesopotamia having some of the famous biblical stories contained in it a long time before the stories were even thought about for the bible.

While it is easy to provide reasonable doubt that makes Christian mythology glaringly false, many of the stories, deity myths and base moral ideas are repeated in every culture. We can look at this fact and think it is simply because man likes telling stories, or we needed to find a way to describe natural events. Explaining an earthquake to a child as Loki struggling with the venom being dripped on him may be much easier than explaining the sudden shifting of tectonic plates and slips on faults.

It is difficult to see the similarities between these deities and their myths without lumping them all together and choosing to believe that every culture is talking about the same beings with cultural differences. There's no way to prove that line of thinking wrong nor should it be viewed as completely damaging to one to study that as an option. However, when you can notice these things and the differences while preserving the cultural integrity, a whole new side of esotericism opens up for you.

Many believe that Odin is the same deity as the Egyptian Set, the Gothick God (which is hard to deny as the same entity as Odin/Wotan), the Greek Prometheus, the Christian Satan and the Islamic Iblis. If you ascribe to a purely reconstructionist point of view regarding paganism, this way of thinking will seem like blasphemy or unfaithfulness. However, if you cannot see the similarities in the pan-cultural view on numerology, you are left with a small box of ideas from people who think and look exactly like you. This does not fit with the path of an occultist. Granted, taking this too far and becoming another Crowley or making up new-age ideas like Wicca isn't necessary either.

Finding a faith, worship routine or spiritual path that makes sense is daunting, which is why many find out what their ancestors or family friends believed and head that way. However, forcing yourself to fit into a box like "Asatru", "Heathen", "Pagan" or "Odinist" isn't a requirement for someone studying European mythology or someone following or worshipping the Germanic or Scandinavian Gods. You can also be interested in more than one pantheon purely academically or otherwise.

Read from Greek and Roman sources, Middle Eastern and Teutonic sources, Asian and African and everything in between. Study the oracles and sages throughout history and find the common sayings and ideas. Afterward, every religious order you can find, look into that also. You do not have to agree with something to understand it. Studying them all will only strengthen your knowledge of the occult.

When it comes to European lore, like any religion or spiritual idea, study is of absolute importance and understanding cannot come from a biased source nor can it come from a singular source. This is not unique to any religion or belief. If anyone ever says "this is the only way you can learn this" or "read this book but not that book" they are either attempting to control a narrative or sell you something, material or otherwise. Only you can decide what to consume intellectually and what to avoid and only you can make the distinction between what is helpful to you and what is not.

Alchemy of the Gods

C.E. McCann is an Occultist from the United States specializing in Northern European magical practices. She has been practicing and studying magic and the occult for decades and teaches classes on a variety of subjects: Esoteric rune theory and operative rune work, occult philosophy and practice as well as spiritual alchemy. In her spare time she knits and goes camping with her family and kindred.

The Three Little Sisters

The Three Little Sisters is an indie publisher that puts authors first. We specialize in the strange and unusual. Our books are written by long time practitioners, academics and more.

https://shop.the3littlesisters.com

Milton Keynes UK
Ingram Content Group UK Ltd.
UKHW020200091224
452130UK00019B/161